THE FAMILY
IDEA
BOOK

Honey —   4-27-81

this book is for
you because you
really care
about the
family and
because I
appreciate you
for this.
I love you
much
Susan

THE FAMILY IDEA BOOK

Mina S. Coletti
and
Roberta Kling Giesea

Deseret Book Company
Salt Lake City, Utah
1980

© 1980 Deseret Book Company
All rights reserved
Printed in the United States of America

Library of Congress Cataloging in Publication Data
Coletti, Mina S   1945-
   The family idea book.

   Includes index.
   1. Family—Religious life—Miscellanea.   2. Children
—Management—Miscellanea.   I. Giesea, Roberta Kling,
1944-   joint author.   II. Title.
BX8643.F3C64   649'.7   80-10921
ISBN 0-87747-813-9

CONTENTS

PREFACE

President Spencer W. Kimball advises all women to "learn all you can. Growth comes in setting goals high and reaching for the stars." The role of a righteous, successful mother is glorious and noble, especially in these latter days. However, the task is at times overwhelming, and successful motherhood does not come easily or naturally, without effort and perseverance. To make this task easier for the Latter-day Saint mother who understands the eternal impact her example has on her children, we have compiled this reference book. It is a consolidated collection of successful solutions practiced and submitted to us by hundreds of LDS mothers in answer to questionnaires we sent out.

No mother is experiencing complete success in every aspect of family life, but every mother is successful in some area. We've become convinced that there is a reservoir of strength in this record of successful ideas practiced by Latter-day Saint mothers. It is our hope that this book will become an inspirational as well as an indispensible guide to mothers everywhere who are striving to "reach for the stars."

SABBATH DAY

"Remember the sabbath day, to keep it holy.

"Six days shalt thou labour, and do all thy work:

"But the seventh day is the sabbath of the Lord thy God: in it thou shalt not do any work, thou, nor thy son, nor thy daughter, thy manservant, nor thy maidservant, nor thy cattle, nor thy stranger that is within thy gates:

"For in six days the Lord made heaven and earth, the sea, and all that in them is, and rested the seventh day: wherefore the Lord blessed the sabbath day, and hallowed it." (Exodus 20:8-11.)

1

KEEPING THE SABBATH DAY HOLY

Sacrifice

My husband sets the example in our family of honoring the Sabbath through sacrifice. During the week he will work late shifts that no one else wants in order to have Sundays free to worship as he should.

Spirit of Sabbath

My job requires me to work on Sunday once a month. I find that I can keep the Sabbath holy in my heart by "singing" hymns in my head while working, reading and contemplating the scriptures during my breaks, and radiating a spirit of love the entire day. If I keep the intent in my heart pure, I know the Lord will bless me.

Sunday Emergency Kit

I covered a large box with contact paper and labeled it my "Sunday Emergency Kit." In it are items that will prevent me from having to shop or search frantically on Sundays for last-minute "necessities." I'll buy the things on sale and forget about them until I need them on Sundays. Included are the following items: safety pins, extra diapers, spare pairs of nylons, medicine samples, deodorant, makeup, boxed snack items (for drop in guests), and toilet tissue.

Saturday Checklist
Sunday chaos has been replaced
with serenity ever since we
started using the Saturday
checklist system. We won't go to
bed Saturday night until all
items have been checked off.
Everyone helps on Saturday
because as soon as it's complete,
we'll have a family fun time.
Our list is as follows:
Homework complete—Older
children
Fill gas tank—Dad
Wash clothes—Mom
Shine shoes—Older children
Prepare casserole & salad—
Mom
Set table—Younger child
(bowl is set on top of dish; use
two sets of silverware: one for
Sunday breakfast, one for
dinner)
Dust, vacuum—Older child
plus one younger
Scrub bathroom—Older
child plus one younger
Pack diaper bag—Older
child
Bathe all children—Dad
Set Sunday clothes out for
each child

Blessing
My husband had trouble finding
a job because he refused to work
on Sunday. We prayed and
knew we were making the right
decision. We were eventually
blessed when he was offered a
supervisor's job because the
owner respected Mormons and
wanted someone he could trust
in that position.

Church Purse for Little Ones
We have a big "church purse"
that is *always* packed with quiet
toys for the little ones. When we
leave for church, all we have to
do is toss it in the car.

Box Lunches
I fix special box lunch snacks
each Sunday containing treats
that would cause the children to
anticipate the day's main meal.
When I have time, I'll decorate
the boxes in crazy ways.

Lunch on Way Home

My Sundays have become a joy since I started fixing sack lunches to be eaten in the car on the way home from church. There's no kitchen mess and I can relax to meditate when we arrive home.

Meditation

Before leaving for church I provide each of my children some time for individual prayers and meditation. I ask them to think of anything they may have done during the week to hurt anyone's feelings or to disobey rules. They are then asked to discuss these matters with their Father in heaven in the spirit of repentance.

What Can I Do?

Before each meeting, on the way to church, we discuss what we can do to make the meetings better. We can greet people with love, be reverent during the sacrament, and say silent prayers to help the speaker. On the way home we will discuss what we actually did.

My Own Scripture

My children enjoy playing a scripture game when they first wake up in the morning. They each take a turn flipping the scriptures open at random, closing their eyes, and pointing to a verse. This is their scripture for the day. It's inspiring to see how each scripture suits each person to guide him through the day.

Appreciate Beauty

While we travel to church, we view and discuss the beauty of nature. We enjoy taking the leisurely route around the bay because we see everything from seagulls to ducks to sailboats. Our hearts fill with delight and appreciation for such beauty.

Learning Hymns

We sing hymns around the house as we prepare for church. I feel particularly proud of my children when they sing in church because we've learned the words at home.

Heavenly Father Is Our Guest

When my children fuss about bathing and getting "all dressed up," I'll say, "This is Heavenly Father's day. We want him to be proud of us, so we must look and feel our best. Let's pretend he's coming to visit us today."

Sunday Best

I allow my children to decide what to wear between given alternatives on weekdays, but Sunday is my day to choose. I have their clothes ready and laid out the night before. No longer do we have to suffer that last-minute rush to find a missing shoe or to iron a rumpled shirt!

Little Ones Get Messy

My little ones always got dirty before we left for church. Now I have them bathed and combed but undressed when we get into the car. Older children dress them on the way to church. Everyone's busy in the car so I drive in peace!

Dad's Old Shirts

My children wear Dad's old shirts buttoned down the back over their Sunday-best clothes. I don't allow them to take them off until we arrive at the church, so they remain clean and neat. Alternative: Cobbler aprons made from vinyl cloth also work well.

Spiritual Mood

We feel that a spiritual mood is important in our home on the Sabbath. In order to set the tone, we play on the stereo music that is in keeping with such a mood. Any crankiness is quickly dispersed with such music—even my own!

Sabbath Prayers
We know it is important to have Heavenly Father's help in keeping the Sabbath holy, so we remember to kneel as a family in gratitude to ask for assistance throughout the day. The inspiration we receive has been a source of strength to us.

Scriptures and Milk Shakes
Sunday breakfast for our family has become a milk shake with egg beaten in. I read the scriptures to the children while they quietly sip on their shakes.

Family Day
We try to make Sunday a family day. Each week we plan ahead for the next Sunday. We might play scripture games, work on genealogy, or visit shut-ins. Everyone writes down suggestions and then we come to an agreement.

CHAPEL REVERENCE

Sit Together as Family
In order to enforce the counsel that we sit together as a family in church, I tell the children that disobedience means sitting with me at home the next time they want to go somewhere. Even though it is painful, the rule is enforced. Result: Our teens are not loitering in the hall or sitting with a group of friends.

Space Between Children
With eight children, I know that there are one or two who make more noise than others when they sit together. I space them so those two are *not* sitting next to each other during the meetings.

Front Row
I insist that my family sit as close to the front row as possible. There's something about being so close to those looking down at us that causes my children to be reverent. We all feel more a part of the meeting when we can see clearly.

Sitting with Dad
Because my husband is the bishop, we don't get to see him very much on Sundays. However, he always has room on his lap for one child during meetings. Each child looks forward to his turn on the stand with Dad.

Distraction

When my toddler starts making noise in church, I try to distract her by whispering in her ear. I may say, "Look at the sweet baby over there being so quiet," or "The people in that row don't want you to make noise because they can't hear the speaker." Most of the time she listens and settles down.

Understanding

My children seem to behave better in church when I guide them to understand what's happening during a meeting. I may whisper, "That's Johnny's mommy speaking now. She's telling us about family home evening. Let's listen to her."

Discouraged?

Sometimes I find that my children are so busy and require so much of my energy during meetings that I don't gain an uplifting feeling at all. In fact, I'm angry and upset and wonder sometimes if I wouldn't be better off staying at home. I've learned that my attitude often causes such behavior. When I accepted the fact that there would be discouraging days, I was better able to cope with the situation. My children are learning to be reverent step by step, just as they learned how to walk. There's no better place to learn it than in church!

Think Ahead

I always remind my children to make rest room and drink trips before church meetings so they have no excuse to leave the chapel.

Quiet Time

During the week I try to point out to my children the difference between quiet time and talking time. I'll place my finger to my lips and remind them it's quiet time during the meetings. My three-year-old did the same thing to my baby when he was fussy in church, so I know he understands!

9

Leaving the Meeting

When my preschoolers misbehave or get noisy during a meeting, I take them to sit still in a room without toys or distractions. When a certain amount of time has passed, they promise to behave and we return to the meeting where they may play with quiet toys. Allowing them to play in the hall only encourages misbehavior.

Praise—Reward

I find that praising my little ones ("My, you were such a quiet child today") and perhaps giving a reward for good behavior ("You may have a cracker if you can be still until after the sacrament is passed") is effective in promoting reverence in church.

Individual Flannel Boards

I made miniature flannel boards out of cigar boxes for my small children to take to sacrament meeting. The inside lid is the flannel board and the box contains felt cut in various shapes and sizes.

Respect for Sacrament

My children have difficulty sitting still during the sacrament. In order to encourage respect for it, I will not allow toys, books, or other amusements before the sacrament is served. Afterward, they may play quietly if they are too little to listen to the talks. During the sacrament I am reverently praying. I expect them to pray also about the promises they are making to obey God's commandments and always remember him.

Draw Pictures of Topic

My toddlers settle down when I ask them to draw pictures of the people sitting around them, or of something mentioned in the talks.

Help Needed
When my husband was bishop I had seven little children to keep in line during the meetings. He recognized my need and asked a teenager to aid me during sacrament meeting. I could then take care of the baby without having to worry about the preschoolers.

Snugglers
We take quilts to church so that when the little ones get tired, they have a comfortable place to snuggle.

Reverence Monitors
My children have been encouraged to be reverent in Sunday School and sacrament meetings by either watching or being reverence monitors. Our ward had a problem with reverence until this idea was initiated. A girl and boy stand in front of the chapel facing the audience with their arms folded until everyone is seated in the chapel.

Quiet Toys
I find the following to be excellent church meeting toys:
—magnets
—small locks with keys
—pipe cleaners, which can be twisted into animals, shapes, and people (crumpled aluminum foil can also be twisted)
—pen and paper
—*Friend* magazine
—magic slate
—old jewelry
—quiet books

Church Snack
I string Cheerios for a nonspillable baby's church snack.

Morse Code
I taught my children the Morse code to be used in place of whispering only when it is *necessary* to communicate. If done softly on a hymnbook, no one else can hear it.

11

Express Gratitude
I set an example and encourage my children to express gratitude to the speakers for their talks. When they give a talk, they enjoy praise and understand its importance.

Listen to Talks
In order to encourage older children to listen to church talks, I have them count how many times a word is repeated, such as "blessing" or "Holy Ghost." At the end of the meeting we compare numbers to see if we all agree. Variation: Everyone writes down three sentences word-for-word to be discussed and compared after the meeting.

No Toys
When our children reach baptism age, they are no longer allowed to bring toys to church. They are expected to listen to the talks.

Report
On the way home from church, I will ask each child in turn what he learned in church that day. If he says "nothing," I will ask him to read from one of the church magazines and report to us something of value he has read. Each person now listens so he can report on the meeting.

Too Young to Fast
Sometimes a little child may find it difficult to maintain a complete fast on fast Sunday, so I'll suggest that he give up something (such as dessert) instead. When he reaches baptism age, he is then expected to fast in the normal manner.

Not Singing

Not too long ago I realized my eight- and ten-year-olds were not singing the hymns in church. I warned them that they would be spending one-half hour at home each day practicing singing if they didn't know how to sing. It worked. They've been singing ever since!

Never Criticize

I never criticize the meeting, speakers, or others on the way home from church. Instead, I will try to mention the main ideas expressed in the talks and encourage my children to express their feelings. I've been able to clarify misunderstood points in this manner.

SABBATH ACTIVITIES

A Family Day

From the time they were small, my children have not been allowed to play outside on Sunday, nor can they have the neighborhood children over as they do the rest of the week. They say, "This is a family day," when asked why they can't play.

No Shopping

When the children asked why we don't shop on the Sabbath, I took them to observe a supermarket and department store. We noticed how people dressed and asked ourselves if they were happy or if the spirit we find in church was there. We then read the scriptures pertaining to the Sabbath and explained that we choose to obey the counsel of the Lord.

Quiet Day

We encourage our children to spend quiet time in their rooms between meetings. They can read, write letters, sleep, work on journals, or do other quiet things. The house is to be quiet and relaxing for all. They don't play outside or go on outings unless it is to visit someone who needs cheering.

Testimonies

We have a tradition of having our own testimony meeting as soon as we get home from fast meeting. Whoever didn't bear a testimony in church does so at home. We ask family members to explain how Christ influences their lives. Once they open their mouths, a beautiful spirit fills our hearts, uniting us in a sacred experience.

Secret Pals

We have family secret pals who do something nice for each other on the Sabbath day, such as secretly placing notes or treats in the pal's bedroom. Coupons offering to do a chore for the pal may be given. During family home evening the pal is identified and a new one drawn. Mom and Dad participate also!

Prepare Lessons

I often have handouts or favors to make for my Relief Society lesson. Sunday is a good day for me to prepare these. I have the children help me cut, staple, and glue. I discuss with them the ideas in my lesson while they help. They sometimes have worthwhile suggestions for me.

Scripture Messages

My children enjoy making scripture messages out of old magazines or newspapers. Each cuts out words to form a scripture. The others have to guess the standard work, book, and verse from which it comes.

Save Sunday Newspaper

We enjoy the Sunday newspaper but feel that reading it is not in keeping with the Sabbath. We merely put it away until Monday or sometimes buy it Saturday night to read then.

Sunday Puzzles

We make special Sunday puzzles from discarded library pictures or those found in old church magazines. Pasted onto cardboard, they can be saved in envelopes to be used over and over again.

Red Light—Green Light

I showed my children a picture of a stop light with green, yellow, and red lights. I asked them to tell me which activities I read from a list were acceptable or unacceptable on the Sabbath day by responding with the words "green light" or "red light." I discovered what they knew and where their weaknesses and strengths were in keeping the day holy. Now, whenever they ask to do something, I'll ask, "Is it a red or green light?" They usually know the answer.

Find the Object
Some Sundays when I know my children are trying to keep a good spirit in the home but are restless, I treat them to a long indoor treasure hunt. I set items within sight in the living room, hand the children a list of the items, and tell them they are to record where each item is without touching or moving it. When they finish they write why these things are important to us as a family. Other times a quiet hunt leading to a snack is a way of relieving boredom.

Family Letters
We spend time between meetings writing family letters to a missionary from our ward or to grandparents. We vary the stationery we use. One time we wrote on a whole roll of toilet paper. Another time we wrote on the back of the children's art work. We've written in circles, with double pens, and in "secret ink."

Rest Home Sacrament
As a family, we volunteered to take the sacrament to a sister in a rest home. My husband and oldest son blessed and passed it while the rest of the family knelt around her bed. One of our younger children recited the sacrament gem while another told her the main ideas taught in either the Sunday School or sacrament meetings. We became so attached to this sister that each of us has lingering memories of those visits.

Hitch-a-Ride Seeds
We feel that a leisurely stroll up the street is quite in keeping with the Sabbath as long as our hearts are intent upon worshiping Heavenly Father with gratitude for his lovely blessings. Just for fun, I told the children to pull a fuzzy old sock over one shoe on one such walk. As we walked along we picked up many "hitch-a-ride" seeds and leaves. When we arrived back home we discussed these seeds and related them to God's eternal plan.

Mom and Dad Do Dishes
Because our children do the dishes all week, Mom and Dad give them a sabbath day rest by doing the dishes for them. Sometimes we even use paper plates and cups to minimize the work.

Wisdom Recipes
Our "Family Recipes of Wisdom" booklet was a special family project for Sunday afternoons. We each designed, worded, and added a page to the book every Sunday until it began to bulge. Whenever we'd learn a gem of wisdom, we would think of a clever way to word and illustrate it for the book. For example, one reads "A screaming house is not a happy house," while another reads "An apple a day keeps the sugar away." Even the preschoolers are clever in their thinking. One day my three-year-old said, "The Holy Ghost is Heavenly Father's sheriff."

Songfest
Our family will occasionally spend time singing appropriate hymns and songs around the piano on Sunday night.

Family Firesides
Our family started a tradition of having firesides every Sunday night. We may discuss topics of interest, play games, or just quietly read the scriptures in one another's company. Popcorn is a traditional snack.

Fellowshipping
We try to fellowship the new members of our ward. Sunday is a good day to invite a new family over for a simple meal or dessert—prepared on Saturday, of course!

Ice Cream Snack
Our family looks forward to eating ice cream sundaes every Sunday evening.

Scripture Snuggle
Sunday night everyone snuggles together on Mom and Dad's bed to read scriptures. We may read several consecutive pages or we may select one or two passages to discuss and ponder.

Sabbath Day Irritations
I have discovered three sources of irritation on the Sabbath day and have eliminated them:

1. Sunday newspaper— scattered all over, people reading it instead of spiritual books. Solution: cancelled it.

2. Sunday meal fixing and cleaning. Solution: Traditional lunch is pancakes. An assortment of toppings makes it interesting. Dinner is hot dogs, toasted cheese sandwiches, or canned soup. Children fix it themselves while Mom is at choir practice.

3. Television brought the world and laziness into our home. Solution: No TV at all. Our stereo playing the Tabernacle Choir or other appropriate music sets a spiritual mood while we pursue our quiet Sabbath endeavors.

But, Mom, Why Can't I . . .
When my children desire to do something that is not in keeping with the Sabbath, such as riding bikes, I will say, "You really want to go bike riding, don't you? We'll have to schedule it into the other six days of the week. Which day do you want to go?"

Birthday Parties
My children are constantly being invited to birthday parties on the Sabbath. We always turn these invitations down with the excuse that we want to keep the Sabbath holy. My children have been disappointed several times, but a reward finally came when one little boy said he planned his party on Saturday so my child could go this year!

Do-It Jar
A Sunday "do-it jar" is helpful in directing our children to their day's activity. Filled with written suggestions of what to

do, the jar is decorated with contact paper. Each Sunday an idea is drawn and put into practice. Ours contains the following ideas:
—Rest.
—Plan family home evening assignment.
—Make up a scriptural crossword puzzle.
—Learn a church hymn.
—Play "who's who" in the scriptures—give clues about scriptural character and have someone try to guess who it is.
—Copy genealogy charts.
—Go for a walk. Return with a list of nature's blessings.
—Look at pictures of ancestors and learn of one to talk about in family home evening.
—Record in journal or book of remembrance.
—Write letter to grandparents or missionaries.
—Ask parents to interview you.
—Do a good deed for someone.
—Draw pictures of your blessings.
—Make a gift for the bishop or teachers.
—Read *New Era* or *Friend* magazine.
—Write a short story about an uplifting experience.

—Cut a paper doll family out of an old magazine and play with little brother. Have the dolls show him how to be kind and considerate to family members.
—Visit someone in a rest home or hospital.
—Gather flowers to surprise Mom.
—Read *Children's Book of Mormon* or listen to tapes.
—Create a test on the Book of Mormon to be given in family home evening.
—Memorize the Articles of Faith.
—Write your testimony in Book of Mormon to be given to investigators.
—Lie down on the lawn in order to spend five or ten minutes talking to Heavenly Father. Be certain to quietly listen for an equal amount of time.
—See if you can make a list of answers to these questions:
1. Why do I keep the Sabbath day holy?
2. What are some ways to show love to my parents?
3. Why do I want a temple marriage?
4. How can I be a peacemaker?
5. What are the advantages of being a Mormon?

Book of Mormon Testimony

In order to contribute to the Church's missionary effort as a family, we purchased several copies of the Book of Mormon. One Sunday afternoon we individually included a testimony, as well as our address and a snapshot of our family, in each book. We then sent them to the mission president to be distributed to investigators. As a pleasant surprise we've received letters of gratitude from some of those who received them.

Search and Share

We have a Sunday game called "search and share." Each person draws a topic from a hat, then searches through books, magazines, and old lesson manuals for twenty minutes. When time is up, each person gives a 2½-minute talk on his subject.

FAMILY HOME EVENING

"We promise again that as you faithfully plan and hold quality family home evenings, you will gain strength to withstand the temptations of the world and will receive many blessings which will help qualify you to enjoy your families through eternity in the Celestial Kingdom." (First Presidency, *Family Home Evening Manual,* 1978, p. 2.)

PLANNING FOR QUALITY

Buried Treasure
When we receive a new family home evening manual, we choose a theme for the year and each person selects goals. We bury a box containing schoolwork, photographs, and goals in our backyard or favorite campsite. In August we unbury our treasure to see how much progress we've made. We then celebrate with a party.

Seat of Honor
The person giving the lesson sits on an antique chair, handed down from grandfather, which we call the "throne." He is the honored one this night.

Order of Procedure
A chalkboard or poster chart listing the order of procedure has helped bring organization into our family meetings. We rotate assignments so that everyone participates. Example:

Conducting: Bobby
Opening Prayer: Mom
Family Business: Dad (includes allowances, week's schedule, and special problems.)
Opening Song: Jean
Lesson: Vickie and Todd
Activity: Spencer
Refreshments: Mom and Sarah
Closing Song: Jean
Closing Prayer: John

Tired? Busy?

We knew family home evening lessons were important, but we were too tired or too busy to plan them creatively. Now, after committing ourselves to planning the lessons on the Sabbath during a specific half hour every week, we have finally been able to enjoy the lessons. We rotate teaching between Mom and Dad and the children who read. Little ones become assistants in both planning and teaching.

Monday Is Ours Alone

We received joy in sharing our family home evenings with another family, but soon discovered that we really needed the time alone as a family since this was the only night we were together. Now if we want to share an evening, we choose a different night, such as Saturday or Sunday.

Varied Location

Occasionally we vary the location of the family meeting. Some places we've met are:
—Outside on the lawn
—Around the kitchen table
—In a circle on the floor
—In one particular child's room
—On Mom and Dad's bed
—On the "Smith family train" (chairs lined up in a row)
—At the "Smith family zoo" ("animals" kneel behind slats on chair)
—At the city park

Bulletin Board

In order to draw attention throughout the week to the message of the previous lesson, we have a family home evening bulletin board. All week we see pictures, scriptures, and key words pertaining to the previous lesson. The person who teaches hangs his material on the bulletin board when his lesson is over.

Lesson Manual

We're delighted and inspired by how helpful and well-planned the lessons are in the family home evening manual. To complement the current manual, we often refer to the wealth of clever ideas, games, and stories available in at least ten outdated manuals.

Ward Library

Our family home evenings became more interesting when we started using the ward library facilities. Filmstrips, pictures, flannel boards, and books paved the way to creativity in our lessons.

Focus on Manual

The lesson manual rests in a place of honor on our hall table. All eyes are drawn to it when I set an attractive flower arrangement next to it. It's surprising how it opens up conversations about the Church with our nonmember friends. Also, everyone knows where to find it when they need to prepare a lesson.

Family Needs

We have found it very effective to handle some issues naturally under religious auspices of family home evening rather than making problems of them at another time. Such topics as sex or popular music may be discussed in place of the lesson in the manual as our family needs demand.

Selecting Lessons

On the first Monday night after fast Sunday, we select the four lessons for the month by reading the topics in the manual and voting on those to be covered that month. Assignments are also made so that those who will teach will have plenty of time to prepare.

Reinforcement

Each week we set aside time to review the previous week's lesson. We ask for examples of how the message helped us during the week.

Phone Policy

If the telephone interrupts our family night we say, "Hello, family home evening."

I'm Busy Monday Night

Many activities are scheduled for Monday night outside the Church. When we finally made an inflexible rule that couldn't for *any* reason be broken we were able to have everyone present for family home evening. We advised our children to say "I'm busy Monday night" if asked to go elsewhere.

No Husband Monday Night

My husband works on Monday nights. After not having family home evening for years, we committed ourselves to holding Sunday night home evening. We have to plan thoroughly ahead, but we find we are able to have a more closely knit family and a spiritual Sabbath.

Nonmember Husband

Because my husband is not a Church member, I thought it would be impossible to hold family home evenings. Once I made up my mind to have them without him, I found that it wasn't an impossibility after all. At first I merely held a family game night without calling it family home evening. Not realizing it was church-related, my husband soon joined us in the fun. Now we've added a simple lesson and my husband does not object. In fact, he's learning about the Church, too!

Mom and Dad Time

My husband and I have set aside time for each other after the children retire to bed every Monday night. We assess our stewardship as parents, discuss both immediate and long-range goals, and study scriptures together. The sweetness of the house and the unity we achieve have now erased any desire to watch TV or pursue individual interests.

Hymnbooks

When our ward bought new hymnbooks, we were able to purchase some of the discarded ones for our family. We set them out each time we have family home evening. Now no one has an excuse for not singing. Primary songbooks are also used that night. The little ones enjoy leading us in their songs. I should note that even *new* books are inexpensive.

Notebooks with Family Crests

Each member of our family has his own family home evening looseleaf notebook covered with a picture of our family crest designed and drawn by himself. Each notebook contains a calendar and blank paper for recording assignments and points to remember.

Sing-Along

A cassette tape with children's songs helps a nonmusical family "sing along." Songs from Mormon plays and the Tabernacle Choir are also convenient to tape and sing.

Treasured Records

Each week we assign a secretary to take minutes of our family home evening meeting. At the end of the year we have a treasured family journal that helps us recall special moments. One entry reads "Mom had to leave the room to change the baby when he knocked over a vase during Daddy's lesson. Everyone laughed except Mom."

ACTIVITY NIGHTS

Surprise
Anticipation is high when a note is found on the dinner table instructing the family to meet at the front door twenty minutes after dinner. The surprise might be a trip to the movies, nearby park, or swimming pool.

Penny Hike
A penny hike is fun for all ages. When the penny flips to heads everyone turns to the right. Tails means to turn left. The penny is flipped only when choices have to be made. No one knows where it will end, but nature can be enjoyed in any direction.

Design a Quilt
We often have a special family home evening project. Recently we made a family quilt. Everyone drew pictures of family activities with fabric crayons. These individual pictures were transferred onto a sheet with a warm iron. Batting was placed between the decorated sheet and a bottom sheet. We tied the quilt during family home evening.

Talent Show
An excellent family home evening activity is a talent show in which each family member "performs" for the others.

Family Award

Occasionally during family home evening we deliver the "Jones Family Award" to a deserving neighbor for being patient with our noisy brood, willing to loan us an item, or just being themselves. One lady cried when we pinned a simple blue ribbon on her dress. Flowers, homemade goodies, or a picture of our family have served us well for these awards.

Grab Bag

Each member is asked to contribute to a worthwhile item he no longer wishes to possess. All the items are placed in a bag, which is passed from member to member as music is played. When the music stops, whoever has the bag may select a gift or exchange the one he has. The game continues until all have something they like. Hint: it may be wise to add items so the last person has a choice.

Old-Fashioned Night

For family home evening we had an ancestor night. We studied our records and pictures of our ancestors, played old-fashioned games, and ate a snack of homemade taffy and caramel corn.

Shadow Puppet Show

Our children enjoyed entertaining us with a shadow puppet show. Hang a white sheet or large white paper from the ceiling. Turn out all lights in the room except for a flashlight or lamp behind the sheet. People can act out scenes behind the sheet, hands can form shapes, or "puppets" made out of cellophane with a cardboard rim and taped on sticks can be used to tell a story. Background music and narration may be desired.

Spending Money on Food
Our children enjoyed selecting a meal in the grocery store. One was asked to buy vegetables, another bread, another meat, and so on. No one knew what the others would buy, and each had a limited amount of money. The meal was unusual but appreciated by all.

Shopping in a Junk Store
Each person was given two dollars to spend in a junk store. They were able to find interesting items to be given as gifts to people they admired.

Stationery Night
In order to encourage our family to keep in touch with friends and relatives, we provided stamps, paper, envelopes, and colored pencils for all to use. We made a supply of addressed, stamped envelopes and placed them in a convenient spot so that anyone could scribble off a note with ease in the following months. We also made our own personalized stationery and wrote thank-you notes.

Flashlight Tag
Our favorite family game is "flashlight tag." This game of tag is played either outside at night or in the dark with a flashlight. Everyone hides from the person chosen to be "it." After counting to twenty, "it" hunts with the flashlight beam for those who are hiding. The first to make it back to a predetermined goal without getting caught in the beam gets to be "it."

Get in Shape
One family home evening everyone enjoyed was a "get in shape" night. We jogged, exercised together, and ended the evening with a baseball game.

Pots and Pans Band
Our family devised a pots and pans band one night when we marched and danced around the house. Wooden spoons and pots served as drums, pan lids as cymbals, and funnels as horns.

Tour of Churches

We took our children on a Monday night tour of other churches and synagogues. We had studied and were ready to explain the symbols, decorations, and moral beliefs of each. We went home with an appreciation of our own simple buildings and LDS heritage.

Treasure Hunt

I string a long piece of yarn through different rooms of the house starting in the kitchen. The children follow the yarn until they find a treasure at the end. The treasure could be anything from a treat to a message concerning the lesson to the following week's list of chores.

Clues

For an activity, our family might get into the car in order to follow clues dropped at various places, one leading to another, until we arrive at the ice cream parlor, library, or movies.

Gift of Food

We make TV dinners from our leftovers during the week so we can deliver them on home evening night to singles, older people, or shut-ins who really enjoy them.

Family Home Evening Phantom

Everyone enjoys the excitement of leaving goodies on doorsteps and running before being caught. A "Happy Family Home Evening" note indicates the food is safe to eat.

Home Movie Dinner

We have a drive-in movie dinner. Chairs are arranged in front of a screen as Dad takes orders for hamburgers and hot dogs. Food is delivered and family movies are viewed.

Junk Food

Once in a while as a joke, we have a junk food dinner. We discuss proper nutrition and bring out inadequacies of certain popular foods.

31

Sunday Dinner on Monday Night

I used to fix my big, special meal on Sunday. Now I've switched it to Monday so I can relax on Sunday. To add festivity to the evening, I prepare a favorite casserole, roast, or chicken. I'll set the table as if a guest were coming, with china, crystal, fine linen, and candles. I tell the children they are the "someone special." It really has become an anticipated event.

Foreign Meal

We consider mealtime to be a part of family home evening. To add interest we try to plan a once-a-month meal from a foreign country. As we eat the food, we discuss the history or particular customs of that country. We feel education in food is part of our family's learning experience.

Clever Snack

My children enjoy eating pudding cones after family home evening. They are merely ice cream cones filled with homemade pudding. Raisins or coconut make decorative toppings.

Hidden Dots

Because our children enjoy surprises, I'll occasionally give them napkins during refreshment time that are marked with colored dots. The dots correspond with a predetermined code, which I keep. The dots can be used in different ways. Example:

—As a reward

Red dot: bowl of ice cream

Blue dot: stay up 15 minutes late

Yellow dot: Mom will give you 1 hour of her time

Pink dot: Dad will do your chores

—As a request for desired action or a good deed

Purple dot: take baby for a walk

Green dot: play a game with Jeff

Orange dot: straighten the living room

Black dot: help little brother with homework

Library

My husband surprised us on family home evening by taking us to the library. We used the microfilm machines to read the newspapers from our birthdays. Everyone laughed at the old-fashioned clothes and TV shows that were on then. We were able to make copies of the front pages for the children's scrapbooks.

Scavenger Hunt

One night we had a scavenger hunt without leaving the house. Each person had a stack of old magazines from which they cut out pictures of items previously determined.

Slow Race

Now that my children are riding bikes, we've devised safe games to be played on the bicycles during activity time. A paced race in which we see who can take the most time to go a certain distance without touching the ground is fun.

This Is Your Life

We picked an older person from our ward as our own special grandfather. We surprised him with a "This Is Your Life" evening in which he shared his past with us. We have learned to love him, and feel that he has much to offer us.

LESSON HELPS

Visual Aids
Old pattern books make excellent "people" visual aids for family home evening lessons. I usually let my children help cut them out and then display them.

Booklet
One of our most successful family home evenings was when we taught our children about the Word of Wisdom. We had each of them search through magazines to find pictures for a booklet of things good and bad for our bodies.

People Pile
Our preschoolers sometimes need to get the wiggles out, so we have a "people pile." Everyone piles on top of each other on the floor and rolls around.

Fish for Lesson
My children fish for scriptures, lesson themes, or quotations with a pole made from a string tied to a pencil. A safety pin bent into a hook is on the end of the string. Recipe cards, cut so they are wider at the top, have holes punched in the upper left-hand corner. These cards are placed in slats cut on a box lid. Children take turns fishing for the cards, hoping the hook will go through the hole so they can read whatever is on the card.

Quiet Answers

When I teach a lesson I ask everyone a question. They must answer by drawing a picture. No words can be spoken. The older ones may draw cartoons if they choose. We then show them to each other.

Surprise Picture

For an attention getter I put the pictures for my lesson inside a large manila envelope and pull each one out slowly, inch by inch, letting family members guess what it is.

Puzzles

We make puzzles out of different pictures from the family home evening manual, *Ensign, Friend,* and *New Era* to supplement and add interest to our lessons. We glue the pictures onto cardboard and cut it into various shapes. I have found it very easy to make the puzzles too difficult, so I try to be aware of the child's age and cut accordingly. Stored in envelopes these puzzles are reusable for several different lesson topics.

Paper Doll House

I sometimes draw an outline of an open house showing several rooms. I let the children cut objects from magazines and catalogues to furnish it. We also cut out people and glue them to tongue depressors or popsicle sticks for puppets. We will "play house" or role-play a concept that relates to the lesson topic. For instance, if the lesson is on repentance, we will act out a story with the magazine characters in their house that illustrates repentance.

Family Home Evening Bag

Each family member has a happy home evening burlap bag on which I've embroidered his name with colorful yarn. This bag is to be used only for family home evening lesson gimmicks, treats, or special words of praise. The bags can be opened only when the person teaching instructs family members to do so.

Radio Announcer

During one family home evening, we pretended to be on a radio show. The teacher introduced himself by stating, "Ladies and gentlemen, this is Michael Collins here to report on (topic of lesson) . . ." A commercial advertising a certain scripture relating to the topic may even be added.

Puppets

Occasionally we have a puppet teach the entire lesson. "Home Evening Harry," "Suzie Sunbeam," "Perfect Paul," and "Successful Sam" have all visited us. Hint: Puppets can be made out of small paper bags by coloring faces on them and using yarn or strips of paper for hair.

Handouts

I enjoy giving handouts that represent the topic of my lesson. Packets of inexpensive miniature items can be purchased at a cake decorating or craft store. For instance, when I taught a lesson on love, I found a package of plastic hearts to hand out. A lesson on dating included a (fruit) date wrapped in aluminum foil.

Footprints

I have a box that contains twenty-four numbered footprints made out of colored paper glued on cardboard. I use them as tricks to lead the children to an unfinished chore, a special surprise, lesson quotations or stories to read, instructions for next week's lesson, or games to play.

Plastic Tabs

When I started to save the little plastic tabs that sealed my bread, I didn't know I was saving a useful teaching tool. Felt-tip pens write on them and can be erased easily. These little tabs can be strung into necklaces or hidden around the room with messages written on them. The messages may be scripture references or assignments for the following week. I made necklaces listing each individual's good traits on tabs.

Telegram

Everyone listened attentively when our neighbor delivered a telegram stating the main idea of our family home evening lesson. Such surprises as freshly cut flowers, a box of chocolates, or a singing telegram are planned for delivery during future lessons.

Question Box

We devoted one lesson to questions and answers. The questions can be placed in a box during the week to be drawn and discussed during family home evening.

Hidden Object

I sometimes hide an object that represents the main idea of the lesson. When someone moves close to it, I hum loudly. If they move away, I hum softly. When they find it, I ask, "How is this item like our lesson topic?" Since there isn't just one correct answer, I allow them to guess until I feel the topic has been adequately discussed. I then share my thoughts.

Unfinished Story

Imaginations soar when I read part of a story from the manual and ask family members to finish it. Variation: Type up the story leaving out key words (leave a blank space). Have everyone fill in the missing words.

"Guest" Teacher

To add an element of delight for our children during a lesson, we sometimes have a "guest" teacher. All during the lesson Mom or Dad, wearing appropriate attire, claims to be Professor Know It All, Little Miss Muffet, Casey O'Lacy (an elf), or whoever will add delight to little imaginations. The lesson is delivered with the voice tone and mannerisms of this character. It acts as a marvelous attention getter.

Mulligan Stew

Prior to family home evening each family member is told what the lesson topic will be. He is asked to find a picture or object that he feels will represent that topic. During the lesson, each presents his article and adds it to a large soup pan, while stating his reason for selecting it. When everything is collected, the teacher compliments family members for their thoughts and then adds his own. For example, if the lesson is on repentance, someone might bring an eraser and explain that repentance means we are erasing a sin.

Bean Bag Toss

When I teach a lesson, I sometimes keep everyone alert by throwing a bean bag to the person I question. He tosses it back as he answers. A Nerf ball could also be used effectively.

Key to Happiness

A set of keys made of colored paper or cardboard has been a tremendous aid in seeing that a lesson principle is practiced throughout the week. For example, if a lesson is on kindness, love, or happiness, I give a set of ten keys to each family member. The children are told that each time one is unkind to another, he must give a key to that person. The one with the most keys at the end of the week will have the privilege of choosing his favorite dessert and activity for family home evening.

Tree Branch

A bare tree branch placed in molding clay in a jar lid or vase has become a symbol of our family home evening lessons. I use it for tying game prizes on or as a teaching tool on which I might have the message of the lesson written in code for everyone to interpret. Perhaps I may have slips of paper with words to a scripture scrambled so that everyone would have to place them in the correct order.

How Much Have You Learned?
After four or five lessons, we have a family home evening test to see how much we've learned. The family is divided into two teams. Questions are asked of one member of team A and then one member of team B in spelling bee fashion. Those who can't answer correctly have to sit down until one person is declared the champion.

Question—Answer
At the beginning of a lesson, I pinned questions on the backs of each family member. They could ask anyone else to answer the question without telling them the question. It was up to them to guess the question from the answer they received.

Act Out a Story
The family home evening manuals have excellent stories to illustrate the lessons. We often will assign our children the privilege of acting them out in skit form during the lesson. Simple props and costumes are encouraged.

World's Way vs. Lord's Way
We cut out articles in magazines and newspapers that illustrated the "new morality" of the world. We then cut out articles from church material showing the Church's stand on these issues. A discussion of the differences with emphasis on the Lord's way gave our children a deeper insight into the deception of the world. It also cleared up confusion within them.

Deception
In order to illustrate how deceptive Satan is, I baked a cake and decorated it to appear lovely and delicious. I left out the sugar, however, so when I gave everyone a taste they were surprised to find that it did not taste as delicious as it appeared.

Pop Balloons

Balloons aid me in giving family home evening lessons. The children love to pop them in order to read a message within. The message can be directions pertaining to the lesson; for example, messages may read: "Read John 4:11," "Role-play what you would tell your son if he asked to go out with friends on Monday night," or "Go over and give Dad a kiss." If I, as a teacher, know which color balloon holds which message, I can let them be popped one at a time as they fit into my lesson plan.

Sing to Memorize

We've decided to memorize the books of the Bible, so we take turns singing them to familiar tunes. For instance, "Mary Had A Little Lamb" may be a tune used by my daughter, while my son may choose "Row, Row, Row Your Boat," substituting the words, "Matthew, Mark, Luke, and John." We've found it to be hilarious but we're learning at the same time!

Know the Scriptures

To encourage familiarity with the scriptures, we often play scripture games. We might race to find as many unusual names as we can in the scriptures within a certain amount of time. Perhaps one person might read off the name of a book in the scriptures while the others race to see who finds it first. A variation may be to mix up the words of a certain scripture and then race to see who can unscramble it first.

Crossword Puzzle

Filling in a large crossword puzzle adds a bit of mental fun to a lesson, especially when the words pertain to the topic. Sometimes the older children create their own puzzles. A lesson on keeping the Sabbath holy could have this puzzle:

Across:
1. Our covenant to Heavenly Father
5. A book of scriptures
6. Once a month we_____
7. How we should keep the Sabbath

Down:
1. Sunday
2. Conversation with Heavenly Father
3. An ancient prophet
4. We listen to _____
8. Spirit we feel in church

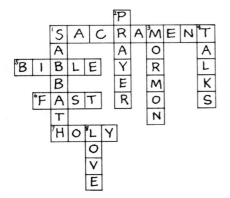

Partners Perform
We found family home evening lessons difficult to teach with children ranging in age from one to sixteen. One solution has been to assign a little one to an older one as partners for a month at a time. The older children are responsible for teaching the younger ones the main idea of the lesson before Monday night. During the lesson the partners perform for the family by illustrating what the younger ones have learned. For example, if the lesson is on sharing, then the younger ones act out the concept of sharing using the older ones to help. Imaginations are exercised and the lesson is learned by all.

Busy Little Hands
We find the age gap in our family is not noticeable if the little ones are kept busy with their hands during the lesson. Such quiet activities as cutting out magazine pictures or creating clay figures that relate to the lesson topic keep them amazingly quiet.

Misbehavior

Our little children often misbehave during family home evening because they need attention. We find that treating them as adults helps them to behave like adults. We ask them questions such as, "Can you tell us what you did when Johnny tried to take your ball away today?" Also, listening to the answer is a must!

Two Lessons

We solve the age-gap problem by first having a very short lesson geared for the youngest children. We then have a snack followed by tucking the little ones in bed. The older children do their homework or prepare themselves for bed until the others are asleep. Then we all meet back for a lesson geared to them. The young ones never feel left out because they don't know we meet again.

Responsibility

Our little children are much better behaved when they are given some responsiblity during family home evening. I sometimes help my child learn a story from the manual in his own words, lead music, hold visual aids, or pass pencils to each member.

Too Young

We didn't hold family home evening because every time we tried our little ones were too young to sit still for a lesson. Since then we've discovered three secrets to solving this problem:

1. Keep the lesson simple and brief.

2. Use varied activities and visual aids, including games, during the lessons.

3. Give them an abundance of attention and love. Be firm but don't get upset with them no matter what happens.

Hidden Lessons

When our family consisted of very little children, we would teach them family home evening lessons on a very informal basis. They often didn't know we had a lesson as such because we would disguise it with play. One night we played house with them. Mom and Dad were the children and they were the parents. We used the entire house as our "playhouse." As we set up a situation and acted it out, we were able to allow our little ones to experience whatever lesson we wanted them to learn. To them, family home evening was a joy because Mom and Dad would "play" with them.

Little Ones Quiet

We save stamps that come in the mail, such as those that come with magazine offers. During the family home evening lesson I allow the little children to paste them into albums (old calendars) to keep them quiet. They enjoy fitting them into the squares.

SPIRITUAL ENRICHMENT

Scripture
We have each child recite a scripture he's memorized before our family home evening meal.

Family Testimonies
One of our special family home evenings occurred when we had each member bear his testimony. Even our one-year-old folded his arms in reverence and mumbled one!

Tapes of Conference
Our church library has tapes of conference talks available to be checked out. When we listen to selected reports that deal with a topic we wish to stress we all have a desire to heed those in authority.

Temples
During a family home evening lesson about temples, we allowed the children to select their favorite temple from an assortment of colored photographs. We then framed and placed them in each child's bedroom as a surprise. We feel the picture will be a constant reminder of our children's goal to enter the temple someday.

Picture of Jesus
We decoupaged a picture of Jesus holding little children on his lap. This plaque has become our official family home evening picture because it sits by our manual during each meeting. Each week we are reminded to mention how much he loves each of us.

Buttons for Reverence
The members of our family learned what reverence meant one night when Dad, without explanation, handed each a roll of buttons (nickels, pennies) before the meeting. Each time someone talked out of turn or acted silly, Dad took a button away without stating the reason. It was fun to watch each in turn figure out why he lost his buttons. As each discerned the reason, the meeting became more reverent. The person with the most buttons at the end of the evening was the Reverence King or Queen. He or she was allowed to stay up fifteen minutes later than usual.

Church Magazines
The *Ensign, Friend, New Era,* and *Church News* play a major role in many of our family home evening meetings. We want to encourage our children to read them when they arrive in our home. Little ones may be asked to recall a story from their magazine, while older ones are asked to share something of interest from their material.

Communication
Sometimes Dad plays "hot potato" with the family in order to open up communication before each lesson. He tosses a potato to someone who will then toss it to someone else as quickly as possible until a buzzer or timer rings. The person with the potato then has the privilege of answering Dad's questions, such as: "What was the most exciting thing you did this week?" "What was the most difficult?" "What do you think of the Word of Wisdom?"

Respect for Prophet
In order to teach the children respect for the prophet, we discuss his conference message as it appears in the *Ensign.* We underline and list points from his counsel so we can apply them to our lives. The children remind us if we fail in certain areas.

Favorite Scripture
Each week one member reads his favorite scripture and then explains why it's important to him.

Reverent Tone

To set a reverent tone for family home evening, we play soft music on the stereo until everyone is seated. The person who conducts chooses someone to offer a prayer. Occasionally we will each talk to our Heavenly Father by taking turns until all have prayed. This helps each of our hearts to be in tune with him. It's amazing how close we feel to one another on those evenings!

Noah's Ark

A rainy day is a good day to have a family home evening lesson about Noah's ark. I especially include the part about the rainbow and God's promise so that his love for us is emphasized.

Scripture Chase

To test our scripture knowledge, we will occasionally have a scripture chase during family home evening patterned after those held in seminary. Little ones team up with older children, offering help by shouting out the chapter and verse.

FAMILY UNITY

Solving Problems

Remembering that one of the purposes of family home evening is to pool our family resources to help one another has enabled us to set aside time during the family business portion of the evening to discuss individual problems. Once I told the family I was concerned about how I would be able to meet the following week's scheduling demands. We brainstormed, allowing each member to offer ideas, suggestions, and even help to solve my dilemma.

Hidden Recorder

A hidden tape recorder has solved many problems in our house. For instance, if children need to learn to speak more quietly or more kindly, I record them candidly and let them listen to themselves during family home evening.

From the Heart

After a week's notice, each person is asked to share something that is special to him. It could be as simple as a teddy bear or as personal as a poem, talent, favorite scripture, or uplifting experience. An explanation of why it is meaningful also must be given.

Special Attention

Occasionally we honor one member of the family. A large poster picture enlarged from a photo of him is a highlight of the evening. Baby book, awards, and compliments as well as his favorite dessert are enjoyed by all. Each member anticipates his own evening of attention.

Fond Memories

The most uplifting family home evening we ever had evolved quite by accident. I had procrastinated putting together my six children's baby books for so long that I had forgotten many of the incidents I thought I'd never forget. We devoted one family home evening to each child. During this time Dad acted as scribe while we brainstormed everything anyone could remember about that child. He felt special and we were knitted together by the bond of fond memories. In addition, I had the needed information for completing baby books.

Profile of Love

Prior to the lesson, shine a flashlight on a person's head so that his shadow falls on a large white sheet of paper hanging on the wall. Outline his profile in pencil or crayon. During family home evening use these profiles to praise each family member. Everyone has to guess whose profile is whose. Kind adjectives such as "full of energy," "considerate," or "discerning" could be used to describe each as hints until the correct person is guessed. When the lesson is over, each person should feel appreciated and loved.

Family Love

Our family received a beautiful feeling of love when we asked each member to state "what my family means to me . . ." during a family home evening. A game could be played by writing answers on slips of paper, mixing them up, and then trying to guess who wrote which one.

Family T-Shirts

Everyone was enthusiastic when we bought a T-shirt for each member of the family stating "Happiness is Family Home Evening." We wear them every Monday night. Variations: Pick a family color and dye or buy T-shirts in that color. Think of a cute saying such as "I'm a Happy Hansen," "Another Great Graham," or "Mama Bell," "Papa Bell," "Middle Bell," and "Baby Bell."

Award Ribbons

Occasionally we honor each member of the family with award ribbons cut from colored paper and decorated with glitter. One may read "Mother's great helper" or "family athlete." The children enjoy being in charge of these ribbons and are quite capable of thinking up clever awards.

Thank-You Time

We look forward to family home evenings because each person is given a moment to thank another member of the family for a kind deed or for just being himself. This not only helps to build each person's self-image, but it also teaches each to express appreciation.

Best Ever Family Chart

A chart with each family member's picture hangs in our family room as a reminder to us to be thoughtful of others. Every time we do something nice for a person outside the family, we add a star on the chart. During "family business" time we discuss who will be the recipient of the thoughtful act for the following week, which may be as simple as sending a card of cheer or as complicated as delivering a meal.

DISCIPLINE

"Parents should never drive their children, but lead them along, giving them knowledge as their minds are prepared to receive it. Chastening may be necessary betimes, but parents should govern their children by faith rather than by the rod, leading them kindly by good example into all truth and holiness." (*Discourses of Brigham Young,* p. 208.)

SETTING THE STAGE

Who Is He?
I try to think of my child not only in terms of who he is now, but of who he was in premortal existence and who he may become. In the face of naughty or bad behavior I keep this mental image in my mind and have faith in his *desire* to do the right thing, whether he chooses the correct action or not. I try to affirm his goodness, feeling that he will become, in large measure, the kind of person I tell him he is.

Increase of Love
Doctrine and Covenants 121:43 states that we should always show an increase of love after reproving sharply when moved upon by the Holy Ghost. As a result of this counsel, we make a point of expressing love to our children whenever they are corrected.

It's Up to Me
I am increasingly aware that as a mother I set the stage for the family. Whatever tone I set will usually be followed by the children. I try to be cheerful even when I don't feel like it because I know that if I blow it and become grouchy the whole household will follow suit.

Close to Spirit
I find that if I live close to the spirit by reading scriptures, obeying commandments, and praying, most of the answers to my questions on disciplining come when I least expect them.

My Stewardship

Whenever my children accuse me of punishing them unfairly or being overly strict, I sit down and tell them of my feelings toward my stewardship over them. I tell them that each morning of their lives I ask Heavenly Father to help me remember that the most important responsibility I will ever have is to bring my children back into his presence. I tell them that I plead with him to help me to be sensitive to their needs, then promise him to do all I can that day to bring this goal to pass. I tell them that I take my stewardship very seriously and that there is no way I could report to Heavenly Father tonight had I allowed them to go to an "R"-rated movie (or to date before age sixteen, to speak disrespectfully to me, or whatever). I have found this kind of honesty helpful in opening their perspective into my role as a loving parent.

Parents Are Team

If one of my children feels I'm unfair, my husband will listen to his complaints as a friend, or vice versa. We never change any discipline decisions without the other's consent, however. We feel it of vital importance to keep the communication lines open.

Apprentice

It helps me in my disciplining efforts to realize that I'm in training now to be a mother in heaven. I'm going to make mistakes, but I can learn by them until I master the problems. The same principle applies to our children in their behavior, so I try to be firm but loving and gentle with them as well as myself.

Admit Mistakes

Whenever I make a mistake as a parent I am not afraid to admit it to my children and apologize. I hope they will follow my example.

DISCIPLINE

Use the Scriptures

To handle behavior problems, I
find that the scriptures are a good
source of instruction. After a
tense situation, I explained to my
son that Heavenly Father loves
him and has given him to me to
instruct him how to behave. We
then read Mosiah 4:14-15
together. He understood and
promised not to repeat his
misbehavior.

Correct Principles—
Govern Selves

Joseph Smith believed in teaching
correct principles and letting his
people govern themselves. I try to
apply this philosophy in our
home. I carefully define a
principle by examples, verbal
explanations, and experience. I
then give my children free agency
to choose a course of action
whenever possible. And they then
suffer natural, logical
consequences that have been
defined previously.

Best Friend

When my son told me he would
be my best friend, I discovered a
new joy. We show respect to one
another and listen to each other's
needs and concerns. He's a
person with feelings, not some
object to dominate.

Children Are People, Too

It took having several children
and enduring considerable failure
before I understood one very
important principle: that children
have feelings like adults, only in
smaller bodies. They should
never be spoken to in a degrading
or unkind way. Now when I have
a discipline problem or am
unhappy with them I always ask
myself several questions: "Is this
the way I would want someone to
talk to me?" "Is this the way I
would talk to an adult?" "Is this
the way I would talk to my best
friend?"

Silent Prayer
I try never to discipline when I'm angry. When I feel anger well up inside me, I take a deep breath of air and offer a silent prayer. Often I will isolate the guilty parties by sending them to their rooms until I calm down.

Aid in Communication
My children and I often kneel in prayer and ask Heavenly Father to aid us in communicating with one another. If we can discuss a problem, each listening to the other, communication is developed and behavior is modified.

No Misunderstanding
Whenever we set rules, we show the children how they should be followed *step by step*. We then ask each to repeat the steps so there is no misunderstanding.

Paying the Price
Every time my child and I have had a disagreement or unkind feelings, and I have knelt for guidance from the Lord, the answer has always been the same: I must be willing to pay the price and not wait for my child. I must make up immediately and not allow feelings of unresolved guilt, anger, or rejection to weigh him down or burden his mind. Time is precious and will widen the gap between us if the problem goes unresolved.

AN OUNCE OF PREVENTION

What Would Jesus Do?
I often ask, "What would Jesus do?" A picture of Jesus is hung above the bed of a child who has been on especially good behavior or has done something especially hard for him.

Switch
I always thought it would be so easy and such a joy to teach my own daughters to cook and sew, but we encountered repeated problems of tempers flaring. I talked to another mother and found she had the same problems. We then arranged to teach each other's children.

Stepped on Soft Spot
We try to teach our children to be aware that there are certain things to which each person will be sensitive. If one says, "You stepped on my soft spot," we know he's been injured in a vulnerable spot and an apology is in order.

Red Flag
We use an imaginary "stress flag" to warn other family members that emotions are strained. If someone says "red flag," we all treat that person with more consideration and sensitivity to his feelings.

Releasing Tension

When I feel tension building up inside myself, I know I'll likely say or do something that may injure my child's self-esteem. I will take a walk, go to my room, or count to one thousand silently until I'm capable of calmly handling the situation.

Warning

If I'm pressured and in a bad mood, I'll warn my children that I may be unreasonable that day. Usually a little rest revives my good nature.

Before There's a Problem

I've found that if I've discussed matters concerning morality before teenage years, it's much easier for my children to accept rules when they are older. For example, my teens have little desire to dress immodestly or to visit unsavory movies because they know that the Holy Ghost will withdraw if a pure environment is not provided for him. They know from childhood experiences that he helps them, and that if they don't encourage his presence, they won't get that help.

Attention

My children seem to misbehave when I don't give them enough individual attention, so I always try to give them some of my time with good nature during the day.

Prevent Inconsistency

To avoid a power struggle with my children, I have a list of rules with punishments attached. They know the consequences for infractions, so I can impose them without being emotional and I'm no longer inconsistent.

Trial Run

I often have make-believe rehearsals with my child before going to such places as the doctor's office, dentist, restaurant, or sacrament meeting. It helps him to be less afraid and to know what's expected of him.

Please, Mother Dear

While my children are little, I teach them to say "please, Mother dear." When others hear them, they offer such praise and attention that the children are motivated to continue using such "fine manners."

Role Playing

I anticipate unpleasant events. In order to instruct the children how to behave, I have them do role playing. For example, I tell them they both want the largest piece of pie. I ask them to act out different ways to handle the situation. I then ask them which leads to happiness.

Sing Your Wishes

One of the sweetest ways a mother can elicit obedience is to gently sing her wishes. I heard a young mother sing, "Please move your little fingers off the table," when she was busy making gingerbread houses. Her child's little fingers were after the candy on the table. He obeyed without question and later was rewarded with a piece of candy.

HE KNOWS I CARE

Running Away
Whenever a child wants to run away, he is generally feeling rejected and unloved. When my daughter told me she wanted to run away, I asked if I could come with her. I suggested silly things we could take with us and soon she was laughing.

Pardons
Occasionally we allow our children to work off a punishment with extra good deeds or chores.

Choices
I give my children viable options when I can. If a child is spitting, I give him a choice: He can't spit in the room or at anyone, but he can spit in the toilet.

We All Make Mistakes
I try to make each major episode that needs correction a learning experience. In one case I told my son when he felt remorseful, "We all make mistakes. It's all right that you made that error. You've learned that behavior hurts people's feelings. Just make certain you don't do it again." This perspective helped lift his guilt. He felt so guilty that he needed no punishment in that case. The error and its result were punishment enough.

Softening "No" with Love
I say: "You're too precious for me to let you play with those scissors. You could cut your sweet little fingers with them."

What Would You Do?

Asking my children what they would do if they were the parents who wanted to teach their children seems to be an effective way to solve a problem. They are often harder on themselves than I would be on them. This method eliminates their feelings of resentment toward me, since they consider their ideas fair. Sometimes we have to negotiate until we reach a just solution.

Momentary vs. Long-Range Goals

I was surprised to realize that I was unconsciously trying to solve surface or momentary problems as they arose. When a child cried, I'd say, "Be quiet. If you keep it up I'll punish you." I was setting momentary peace above the long-range goal of teaching my child how to handle his emotions. Now I look for the cause of the crying and express empathy. "You're really unhappy about . . ." Usually, the crying will stop when he feels love, understanding, and concern from me.

Empathy

I have learned not to feel threatened when my child spouts off with unrealistic expectations. I try to express empathy for what he *feels* his needs are.

Tantrum

When one of my children throws a tantrum, I remove him from us. When he's calm I discuss the situation by showing understanding: "You really got upset because . . ."

Catch the Tears

If a little child cries, I may run to get a glass to see if we can fill it with tears. We hold it up to his cheek and soon he's laughing because he can't catch them.

One, Two, Three

If my children behave poorly in public, I will count on my fingers one, two, three. If I get to three, a punishment will be invoked when we get home.

Consistency

Because my teenagers know I will *not* give an order unless it's important and necessary, they usually mind willingly.

Timed Obedience

When I set my trusty egg timer, the children know they have until it rings to change their naughty behavior.

Guide Him

I have learned that when I want my child to obey, it is a mistake to repeat the request over and over again until it becomes angry nagging. Instead, I walk over to him, perhaps giving him a kiss and gently putting a hand on his shoulder or an arm around his waist, and guide him to obedience. For example, if I want him to get off the swing in order to leave the park, I first tell him it's time to go home. Then, if he doesn't come, I will guide him to the car.

Get His Attention

If a quick punishment is absolutely necessary, I will slap one of my own hands while holding it behind the child's bottom. He hears the noise and feels my displeasure but is not physically touched. I also make certain he understands his misdeed and why he should not repeat it.

You're Doing It Again

I had difficulty with my children being rude. I tried every form of punishment I could devise, but nothing worked until I realized they were copying my tone of voice! It had become an unconscious habit and I was to blame. Now, each time they do it, I just point it out to them by saying, "You're doing it again. Stop, reword it, and repeat it correctly." I also mentally correct myself in this manner. It's working with no punishments attached.

Warning

I have changed threats, such as "Do this or I'll spank you," into warnings—"If you do that you may get hurt." Sometimes my child has to experience the result of his actions, if it isn't too dangerous.

Quietly

Whispering in the ear will usually get the attention of an angry or noisy child.

QUARRELING

Hunger Pangs

My children often started quarreling just before dinner time. When I realized that hunger probably caused unpleasantness, I provided a predinner snack such as sliced fruit, dinner salad, or raw vegetables with a dip.

Retire the Referee

After years of stepping in and trying to help my children solve their differences I became aware that, no matter how fair I thought I was being, the "good" child always looked "good" and the more aggressive, verbal child always looked "bad." Likewise, from somebody's point of view I was always unfair and taking sides.

I began to suspect that this fighting was for my benefit. After considerable thought I decided that for twenty-one days I would completely disengage myself from the "battle front" by refusing to enter in no matter how bad the fighting got. I planned to assess the situation in three weeks.

For a while the fighting intensified. The children tried everything they could think of to persuade me to referee. I would merely say in a disinterested way, "This is between the two of you. I'm sure you can work it out." I held firm, and before the twenty-first day arrived the situation had definitely improved. They still have disagreements, but they no longer "fight" to get my attention.

64

Early to Bed
When there is repeated quarreling among my teenagers, the rule is this: You want to be treated as an adult. Adults solve their problems in a mature way. If you choose to handle your problems in a childish manner, you will go to bed at a child's bedtime. They then *go* to bed, with lights out, at seven o'clock!

Little Sunbeams
When my children are little, I often praise kind deeds by pointing out that the child is a little "sunbeam" who makes Jesus smile or who lights up the room. Sometimes I hear the older ones praising the others in the same manner.

Mother's Attention
Many arguments are started purely for the pleasure of getting mother's attention. If I leave the room ignoring them consistently they will usually subside naturally. I then try to satisfy the need for attention in an unrelated manner.

Sing
Every time my small children start to quarrel I sing and encourage them to join me in "Let Us Oft Speak Kind Words" or any other song that will change the mood.

Not Busy Enough
When my children quarrel I assume they are not busy enough to be happy. I will hand one the broom and the other the furniture polish. As a result, they have learned to disagree peacefully or at least quietly.

Power Struggle
My child enjoys trying to involve me in an argument with him. If he gets me angry, he has won. When I feel my voice rising, I will bite my tongue and try to appear calm. Saying nothing is the best policy until I reach the point of saying, "That's enough. You've had your say and I'm sorry you feel that way." Allowing myself to yield to a power struggle reinforces his desire to repeat the situation. If I stay in control, he will eventually avoid repeating the attempts.

A Bribe?

Every so often, as a reward at the end of the day for not quarreling, my children can reach into "Mother's Grab Bag" for a special surprise. Little treats such as cereal box surprises, old jewelry, or items I find at garage sales for five or ten cents go into the bag as I acquire them.

Taking the Wrong Away

I help my children see that if they keep the other person in the wrong and don't "take the wrong away" from him, they become peacemakers. For example: Often a fight starts by one person teasing. The other retaliates either physically or verbally. But if the person being teased ignores the other, he leaves the teaser in the wrong.

Time Out

When the children get too unruly, I say "time out." They then are to go to a certain place, such as a chair or room. After an appropriate amount of time, they may return to play.

Be a Peacemaker

After reading King Benjamin's admonition in the Book of Mormon (Mosiah 4:14), we do not allow quarreling in our home. When the children are young we spend a lot of time instructing them on how to be peacemakers. When a quarrel arises, they are immediately separated and told to spend the time thinking about what *they* could have done differently. I then discuss the problem individually, acting as counselor to interpret what actually happened. They are to recognize their own error and apologize to each other. When older, I assume they know the principle and can apply it by discussion without my intervention. As a result, if they indulge in quarreling, they automatically lose a privilege, such as the next favor asked of Mother. It's interesting to see how quickly they solve a disagreement peacefully without my knowledge!

TEENAGERS

Teenage Doubts

No one could have prepared me for my first child's becoming an adolescent. I slowly watched him change from a trusting child to one who constantly questioned my views. Once I accepted the fact that this behavior was normal, I could relax in the knowledge that I had adequately prepared him by teaching him as a small child the basic principles that he now questioned. I remembered seeing the belief in his eyes and knowing that he understood. This knowledge gave me comfort, and I prayed that somehow the hours and days during those trusting years would outweigh his days of rebellion. When he finally gained his own personal testimony, my joy was full.

Homework

We've solved our "getting homework done" problems now that I've provided a study time and given my children the responsibility of suffering the natural consequences if it doesn't get done. They have been told that if they wait until bedtime to do their homework (even though they may have a test or paper due the next day), they may not stay up to do it. Bedtime is bedtime. After my daughter suffered her teacher's displeasure once, she knew homework was to be done during study time. I am free from having to nag!

Good-Deed Chart

We have a good-deed chart. For each good deed they do my children receive ten cents; for each incident of trouble, they lose ten cents. Any object of value to children can be used in this manner. Coupons worth "a good deed from Mother" could be used in the same way for teens. It's very effective to be able to say to a teen who has chosen not to do any good deeds, "No, I won't iron your pants at the last minute because you haven't earned any coupons. You made the choice when you decided *not* to earn them." It's interesting to see how willing they are to be helpful when I remain firm and just.

Personal Belongings

With six children I have had the opportunity of trying many different methods of getting the children to keep their clothing and other personal belongings picked up and put away. These are some of the more effective ways:

—Put all uncared for items in a lost and found box. You can either have them pay to get each piece back or, as I have found successful, refuse to give anything back until each Monday night.

—Withhold permission: "you don't go . . ." or "you can't . . . until it's done."

—Postpone any new purchases for the offender until he has continuously taken care of what he already has for a selected period of time.

—Make a complete and detailed list of everything you have done for the child that day, then hand him a blank piece of paper and ask him to do the same.

Being Home on Time

We have three teenagers in our home. Our problem of having them return home at the appointed time has been solved as follows: We discuss together the time the person is to be in, and he sets his alarm clock for the agreed-upon time. My husband and I are then free to go to sleep. All is well as long as he is home in time to push in the alarm button. If the alarm goes off the consequences go into effect without argument.

Waiting Up

I always wait up for my teenagers when they are out for the evening. They know that if they are not home at the correct time I will call them where they are and I will be up when they arrive home. I will listen to explanations and will make the punishment fit the "crime." For instance, if they rob an hour of my time, they then owe me an hour of their time.

COMMON PROBLEMS

Getting to School on Time
To encourage our children to be
responsible for getting ready for
school, we gave the older ones
their own alarm clocks. We told
them they must set them and
get themselves up. If they were
not to the breakfast table on
time, all they would have would
be a glass of milk. If they were
late I would not drive them. The
first week was one of testing
(would I give in?), but after that
it was like a miracle. I no longer
had a problem.

Nagging Mother
When I realized it was better to
be quiet instead of always giving
unsolicited opinions, my
children started coming to me
for advice. Sometimes I've had
to bite my tongue and just let
them learn by experience. For
example, instead of nagging
them to take their jackets, I'm
silent. They soon return for
them after a moment in the
cold.

Misbehaving
I have often found it rewarding
to send a child who has
misbehaved to his room,
suggesting he pray.

Grocery Store Grabbing

When I took him shopping, my young son, who was sitting in the grocery cart, kept grabbing articles off the shelves. I whispered in his ear while lovingly caressing him. Someone nearby asked, "I wonder what you whispered?" I smiled and answered, "I told him to put it back."

Understanding His Desires

I've solved the problem of my children throwing tantrums in a store by merely showing them empathy. For example, when my son finds an item he desires to have, I say, "You'd really enjoy that, wouldn't you?" or "Oh, that looks so good." He responds affirmatively. I then walk with him to the shelf saying, "Let's put it back so it will be there when we decide to buy it." I don't promise him anything, but I don't deny him the natural impulse to dream and anticipate.

Bedtime Blues

We found an instant cure for bedtime crying. One night as my darlings were vocally rebelling at having been put to bed, my husband got out the tape recorder, stood outside their door, and recorded about five minutes of their screaming. Then he went in and started playing it for them very loudly. Their tears turned to laughter.

Mealtime

Each night I bring my children to dinner with a dinner bell. The first time is the warning—"get ready"; the second time we eat. I never yell. If they aren't all around on the second bell they don't have the privilege of eating until after we are finished. If they miss more than once in a reasonable period of time they go to bed without dinner.

Stop the Car

When my children become unruly in the car, I simply stop the car until they calm down. They must make up for the time I waste by doing chores for me.

In the Car
After repeated quarreling in the
car over who got to sit by the
favored window, my husband
and I planned a trip we knew
would appeal to the kids. Then
after about one mile of the usual
fighting we turned the car
around without saying a word
and on arriving home
announced to them that since
they all loved the window so
much, instead of going on the
trip, each one would now have
the privilege of sitting all alone
in the car by the window for one
full hour. We never had the
problem again!

ENCOURAGING GOOD BEHAVIOR

White Bean—Brown Bean

When I was little, my parents kept individual records of our behavior in little glass jars labeled with each child's name. A white bean was dropped into the jar for each good deed, and a brown bean was added for each negative act. Once a week during family home evening our father inspected the jars. Those who had all white beans would be excused from household duties for one day the following week.

Caught in the Act

Instead of spending time looking for things my children are doing wrong, I use the motto, "Catch them doing something good." Reinforcing their good behavior encourages them to want to repeat the correct action.

And for Good Little Bunnies

Reading the story of Peter Rabbit while eating currant buns and drinking warm lemonade is a sweet way of reinforcing behavior in a child who has corrected bad behavior by being obedient.

Report Card Praise

When my children brought home report cards, I wrote each a little note of appreciation for their efforts, praising their positive grades. Slipping these notes under pillows, taping them to headboards, or placing them in lunch bags could add an element of surprise.

Diversion
Diversion of attention works
with my preschoolers. I teach
my three-year-old to give his
one-year-old brother a different
toy when the younger one tries
to take a toy away from him.

INDIVIDUAL ATTENTION

"Like many young men, I once had a paper route; and I had to get up early in the morning to deliver them. One morning I woke up and looked outdoors to see one of those torrential Arkansas downpours. I thought we were in for another flood! As I prepared to go out in that rain, my father came into the room dressed in his business suit. 'Get in the car, Paul,' he said. 'I'll drive you around your route this morning.' This meant he would have to go without his own breakfast. . . . Do you think that there was ever any doubt in my mind as to my father's greatest concern?" (Paul H. Dunn, *Ensign,* May 1974, p. 15.)

DISCOVERING NEEDS

Who Needs Me Today?
I begin each day in prayer to my Heavenly Father. Because I have seven children, I ask, "Who most needs my attention today? I am but one person and can serve one other well today." I feel the answer come, often finding that it's the same person two or three days in a row until we solve a particular problem. Sometimes it's a neighbor or friend, but most often it's one of my children or my husband.

Rock Faces
We collected various-shaped rocks and allowed each child to oil paint an original face on one. When a child has a need for my time, I will find his rock on my nightstand. I then return it personally to that particular child when I have a block of time to spare.

Happy Face—Sad Face
Mood faces aid us in assessing our children's attention needs. Each child has a round circle with a happy face on one side, a sad face on the other. If he is in his room, he hangs either the happy or the sad face on his doorknob. If I see a sad face, I know I must set aside what I'm doing in order to join the child in his room. If two or more children share a room, the faces can be color coded.

Eyeball to Eyeball
To my surprise, one day I discovered I had said "yes" to my son when he asked if he could go on an outing with a neighbor. I frantically searched for him for hours. Later I discovered I had said "uh-huh" absentmindedly in response to his question, while I concentrated on a household chore. I was not listening to him! Now I insist on eyeball-to-eyeball contact by saying, "Look at my eyes," whenever any of my children speak to me.

Busy Teens
It's difficult to squeeze into a busy teen's life, but we feel communication is enhanced by frequent talks. I'll often leave a note in my son's room asking him to set aside time for a walk or ride with me. Perhaps I'll tell him I have a problem and need his counsel. It's been a source of peace to gain from his wisdom!

ATTITUDE

Creative Toys
When I decided to turn off the television and rid our house of unnecessary toys, time for my children was finally available. I will allow them to play only with creative homemade toys. Much of my time is now spent instructing them how to make and play with them. Children are little for such a short time, I know I'm choosing the correct way to spend my time.

Sacrifice
When a child sees us sacrifice for him, he knows that he is loved and is important to us. One mother gets up at three o'clock every morning to deliver papers so she can send her son on a mission.

Keep Promises
A child loses faith in my interest in him if I don't keep the promises I make to him. I never say anything unless I mean it.

Neglect?
I try to remember that time spent with one child who has a need does not make another feel neglected if the other is confident he will receive the same attention when he has a need.

Teach Child to See

I have been a teacher for many years. Often I am asked by young mothers to tell them ways to prepare their children for school. If I could give them one important tip it would be this: Teach your child to see. It sounds simple, but so much depends on it. Take time to be alone with him. Help him to observe, to be curious, to see beauty and then be able to describe what he has seen. This time you spend as you help him develop a love of learning will pay and repay you.

His Needs—My Needs

I will plan my day in the morning fully expecting to be interrupted several times during the day. One time my three-year-old said, "If you play one game with me, I'll let you finish cleaning the refrigerator." If I place *his* needs before *my* need (to have a clean refrigerator), he will learn consideration by my example and both our needs are met.

Ten Minutes

I try to set aside ten minutes a day for each child, just for communication.

Happy Hearts

If I remember that happy hearts are more important than a clean house, our home hums with love. There are some days when housework is not completed because I've joined the children in a game of softball or some other activity.

SHORT SPURTS OF TIME

Childhood Journal
Each of our children has his own set of blank cassette tapes. They may record the day's experiences five minutes before going to bed. When they get older, they may want to type these up as their childhood journal. It will be interesting for them to listen to childhood voices and adventures.

Without Words
Special surprises, such as occasionally completing a child's chores for him, express love and attention without words.

Perfume
A dab of perfume on the back of his hand is a sweet way to help a restless child go to sleep. I instruct him to breathe deeply and think of the things the scent brings to his mind.

Stretch Out on the Lawn
One sunny day I stopped cleaning house to quietly tiptoe outside where I stretched out on the lawn. Before I knew it, the children came one by one to join me. We just lay there enjoying the butterflies, clouds, and grass. I learned much of what was in their little hearts that day.

Rocking Chair
I have an old rocker in the kitchen that has become a symbol of Mom's love. Each morning before I allow my little ones out of the house to play, I will rock each of them silently for a few minutes. Even when they get older they'll say, "Sit down, Mom, I want to rock with you."

My Office
The only way I can be alone some days is to lock myself in the bathroom. When I have something to discuss privately with a child, I will ask him into my "office" for a little chat. One of the other children is assigned to babysit the little ones until we are finished. The rule is, if we are disturbed, we will add ten minutes to our seclusion for each disturbance.

TV Picnic
Occasionally I will let one child plan a picnic, help me prepare it, spread out a large piece of vinyl in front of the TV, and invite the others to join him. They know that it's a special treat and they are always very careful not to spill.

Bad Feelings Eased
One of the best ways I have found to stop bad feelings between myself and a child, or to soothe a child whose feelings are hurt, is to scratch or massage his back. It helps develop a closeness between us, and gives him a sense of my concerned love. There have been times when this was the only method that worked.

LARGE BLOCKS OF TIME

Activities Shared
Jogging, shopping, baking, or sewing can be activities for older children to share with mother. It's important to my children that they are not interrupted, so we provide creative play for the others during that time.

Slave for the Day
One day a month I will be a child's slave for a few hours. He can ask me to do anything from cleaning his room to playing a game or watching TV with him. The rule is that we can't leave our home because we have too many other children to watch. He must be willing to allow me to feed, change, and perhaps hold the baby during that time, but phone calls, visitors, and errands are taboo for me.

Music Lessons
I used to be frustrated because I thought my children kept me from using my musical ability. Now I use my talent in giving lessons to each of my four children once a week! They love the attention. Any talent a mother has, such as painting, dancing, sewing, or playing an instrument, can be taught to a child in a formal way.

Stay Up Later
Individual time is given to my children when each takes a turn staying up later than the others. They respect each other's time because they know they will lose a turn if they are not quiet.

Kitchen Work

I've found that my son enjoys helping me in the kitchen as much as the girls do. With him alone helping me there's plenty of time for kidding around and listening. He needs to learn that it's not "sissy" to be in the kitchen and to enjoy cooking. He will appreciate these skills while he is on his mission and when he's married.

Teach School

I play school with one child at a time. Each child has one turn a week. The others have to honor the time or stand a chance of losing their turn.

Coupons

In order to insure that I would spend time with my children, I gave them each a coupon book at Christmas with twelve coupons, one for each month. The following activities with Mom may be offered:
—Go for a bicycle ride
—Visit the library
—Go for a hamburger
—Take a walk
—See a movie
—Play a game
—Have your back rubbed
I was touched when my son excitedly redeemed a nonmaterial coupon first. He wanted most of all to ride bikes with me!

Exchange Children

In order to have a free day without my children, I tend my friend's children one day a week and she tends mine on another day. Every once in a while I'll keep one child with me so that he will have Mommy alone. Even if I keep him for just one hour by himself, I find his needs are met.

Nap Time

I read or play with my preschoolers before nap time. They know this is their special time with me, so I am able, without guilt feelings, to spend time with the older ones at bedtime.

Trip to City
I treat my younger ones to a trip
to the city on the mass transit
system.

Doctor and Dentist Visits
I don't tell my small children of
doctor and dental appointments
any earlier than necessary. I
always try to accompany a bad
experience with a good one, such
as shopping or going for ice
cream.

Night Errand
One night my son came to me
upset and angry with his father
for reprimanding him. I said,
"Come with me. I was going to
deliver this book to Sister Hall
tomorrow but we can place it in
her mailbox tonight." Just the
fact that I would invite him on a
crazy, middle-of-the-night
errand comforted him, but the
talk we had as we drove soothed
his aching heart. When we
arrived home I knew those few
minutes were well spent because
he was able to give his father a
loving grin before retiring to
bed.

Grocery Shopping
I take a different child each
week to do the grocery shopping
with me. I then allow him to
select one evening's menu.

Car Talks
Many times I've taken my child
for a "car talk." First I'll stop
and get an ice cream cone or
milk shake, then we'll just ride
and talk about things that
normally might be a little
awkward. There's something
about being in a bus or car that
makes the talking easier.
Perhaps it's that we don't have
to sit eye-to-eye, or that long
pauses don't seem as
threatening. Whatever it is, it
has worked well, especially with
my teens and preteens.

Stories of Childhood

I tell my older children little stories about what they did when they were younger. They sometimes forget they received the same loving attention the little ones receive.

Dream Shopping

I have three teenage daughters, and although we don't have a lot of money to spend on clothes from the store, they still love to window-shop. Many times a year I will take one daughter at a time to the shopping mall. My time is all hers and she lets me know about herself as we look only at items suited to her interests.

Bargain

I knew my son was having a difficult time getting his personal scripture reading done each morning. So I asked him how long it took him to straighten his room and make his bed each morning (something he hated to do). He said about ten to fifteen minutes. I made a deal with him: If he would get up and really study the scriptures for the time he would normally spend straightening his room, then I would do his straightening for him. It worked out beautifully. I didn't mind the few minutes of extra work, and it was just the incentive he needed.

IDEAS FOR FATHERS

Breakfast Date
Every Saturday morning my husband takes my three preschoolers out for breakfast so that the older children and I can clean house without interruptions and he can give the younger ones his full attention. Breakfasts for children at certain restaurants are still reasonably priced, so we can afford the luxury.

Buying Presents
My husband enjoys taking the children shopping for a Christmas or birthday present for me. He delights in their joy in selecting "just the right thing for Mommy."

Scheduled Date
Every child has a chance to schedule a date three months in advance with Dad. We then put it on the calendar as a fixed date. The child has the opportunity to express whatever he desires to do with his Dad, and if it's within our means, Dad must do it. My teenage daughter once stated that her heart's desire was to go skiing with him alone.

Work with Dad
Going to work with Dad when he plans a slow day is an adventure our children anticipate. A lunch with Dad near his office is just as exciting to a child, if going to work is impossible.

Monthly Interviews

Our children look forward to monthly interviews with Dad. The first Sunday of the month, when we have no sacrament meeting in the afternoon, is the best time for us to have such interviews.

Family Prayer

When we have family prayer, my husband remembers to mention each child. Individual problems and achievements as well as expectations are discussed with the Lord. This prayer not only teaches who has all the answers, but it makes the individual child feel important and loved as he hears concern for him expressed.

Day with Dad

A delightful afternoon for father and young son is to go around to tractor, motorcycle, and boat stores and pick up catalogues. The little sales books are free and provide weeks of dreaming, cutting, and pasting.

Date with Mom and Dad

A child feels quite important if he is allowed to go out on a date with Mom and Dad. He can be taken out to dinner or to a movie. We alternate so everyone has a turn. Daddy-daughter or mother-son dates are a joy too!

Father's Blessings

A precious time for our children comes when Dad gives them a blessing for whatever they need. It may be to guide them in decisions, calm them in days of stress, or heal illness. This attention lets them know we are concerned for their well-being, builds their morale, and, most importantly, reinforces an awareness of Heavenly Father's love for them.

Sing

My husband will stand by the piano to sing while my son practices. The spirit of love between the two is strong during these short moments.

Time for Bed
When my husband is home to
tuck the children in bed, he will
make up a story about them.
Most of the time it will include
that particular day's
experiences. They look forward
to this special attention from
Dad.

IDEAS FOR BUSY DAYS

Exhausted

I'm usually exhausted at night, so I alternate "sleeping" with each child. When he is in bed I will lie next to him for five minutes or more. I'm silent at first in order to allow conversation to proceed at his pace. Sometimes just knowing I'm there is all he needs.

Changing Diapers

Playing peek-a-boo, singing, or tickling a baby while changing his diapers adds spark and love to his life. It takes no more time to change him, either!

Surprise Dinner

When I need help, I allow my children to prepare a surprise dinner by themselves. We don't know what will be served until it's on the table. I'm usually delighted with how well they work as a team to surprise Mom and Dad. They always receive praise and help cleaning up from us.

Breakfast Cook

A child feels important and I'm free to do other things when he is assigned to cook breakfast all week. He makes the menu, which is then posted on the refrigerator. If I freeze extra pancakes or waffles ahead of time, then even the little ones can participate by using the toaster. If I have time, I will be an assistant who will do as the "chef" dictates.

Not Rejected

If I'm busy when a child needs my attention, I never send him away unless it's impossible to give him time right then. I make certain he doesn't feel rejected by kissing him and telling him when I will have time.

Verbal Attention

Some days are so busy that I don't have blocks of time to spend with my children individually. I then strive to give special verbal attention in the following ways:

1. Questions about their activities or feelings or interests. I may ask, "Sue, what happened in Girl Scouts today?" or "John, what are your thoughts about . . .?"

2. Many times I'll play guessing games with my children while I cook, fold clothes, or iron. My teenagers are responsive to me as we discuss homework, dating, or personal problems while work is accomplished.

3. I give my children attention without spending a lot of time with them when I use pet names such as "My Little Miss America," "Princess," "My Big Man," or "Good Guy."

Radiate Joy

It takes no more time to be happy than it does to be unhappy. Therefore, as each child arises in the morning, I greet him with a big hug and kiss. Even though I may feel grouchy inside, they always know I'm happy to see them. I set the tone, and that's a responsibility I take seriously.

Do You Need Me?

My eight-year-old respected my busy schedule when I said, "Sally, is there anything you need or want to discuss now? I'll be busy for the next few minutes (hours) and won't want to be disturbed."

Morning Visit

When I know a day will be particularly busy, I'll join a child in his room to help him select his clothes for the day, comb his hair, tie shoes, or zip a zipper. If this is handled in a manner of love, calmly and quietly, even the older ones appreciate the help. These moments seem to begin a hectic day with a cushion of love.

91

Where Did You Come From?

I'll often stop what I'm doing to tickle a youngster and ask, "Where did you come from?" in a loving manner. Sometimes they'll say, "Heavenly Father" without even waiting for the question because they know what I'll ask, but I feel the repetition gives them a sense of security and belonging.

I Need Your Help

My children feel very important when I acknowledge their capabilities. I may say, "Spencer, you have stronger muscles than I, could you lift . . . ," or "Heather, you always know which shoes go better with which outfit; could you help me decide . . ." It's surprising how this type of attention gives them an uplifting feeling.

Use of Bath Time

To save time I may read to a child during his bath instead of before bed.

Singing

While I'm working around the house, I may sing an original story about a child nearby. One might start, "Once there was a happy face just grinning at me. . ."

Older Brothers and Sisters

I've noticed that one child may satisfy the need for attention in another. One day while I was canning and had spent little time with my three-year-old, I discovered him fast asleep next to my eight-year-old, who had just finished reading a book to him. I quickly thanked my Heavenly Father for giving us a large family.

SCHOOL DAYS

Lunch Hour
I find that taking a child out for lunch during the school lunch hour is a delight for both of us.

Awaken Early
Occasionally, when I arise early enough, I'll awaken one of my children before the others so that I can be alone with him. I'll help with his morning chores as we discuss what is in his heart.

An Emotional Need
If I feel a child has an emotional need for attention, I will sometimes keep him home from school for a day. After a refreshing and restful day of intimate conversation and quiet activity, I have discovered and eased his needs so that he is ready to return to his normal activity.

A Listening Ear
I always try to be available to each child as he returns home from school. I have a snack prepared and an ear ready to hear that day's happenings.

Surprise Note
When my children arrive home from school, they may find a note on the door to meet me in the family room, garage, or backyard. I may have a game or puzzle set up to play with them, or perhaps I'll offer my time to help them with homework.

OBJECTS OF LOVE

Box of Treasure
My mother has a special box for each grandchild. In it she saves all the letters and artwork they send her. From time to time she adds their pictures and takes the time to write out her own feelings about each one. When they visit her she takes down the boxes and shares the contents. They delight in seeing their first attempts at writing and drawing. These treasured boxes will someday be theirs.

Accomplishment
I feel my time is well spent driving my daughter to gymnastic lessons three times a week. These have given her self-confidence and respect outside the home. She appreciates the sacrifice I make to provide such an opportunity to develop a skill she enjoys.

How Else Can I Be a Man?
It's important to allow our children the opportunity to identify with us. My little boy had been carrying money in his pocket, which he would jingle constantly. When I asked him why he had it with him he answered, "How else can I be like a man?" I allowed him to keep it in his pocket and determined to always provide my children with some object to identify with us, whether it's a purse, a doll, or a set of keys.

Remembrance Flowers
A bouquet of flowers placed on a child's dresser or by his place at the dinner table is a quiet way of recognizing him.

Diary

My five-year-old spent two weeks with her grandmother one summer. Each day she was there Grandma kept a written diary of what they did and where they went. She arrived home with a wonderful booklet that was read and reread and is now part of her book of remembrance.

Photograph Album

From the time my children are born, I order extra copies of each batch of photographs. Some of these are sent to grandma, some are for baby books, and the rest go to make up my child's very own picture book. I buy an inexpensive, self-mounting book (with the transparent plastic pages) and add only photos that include him. This book is his. He can play with it or look at it any time. This provides an excellent aid at story time. It is each child's favorite possession because he can see his growth or reminisce about the past.

Wrapped Gifts Each Day

When my last baby was due I had several small children. To help them avoid feeling left out or lonely while I was in the hospital, I gift-wrapped for each one little presents to be unwrapped one per day until I returned home. I included a doll for each one so that as I cared for my new little one they could work right along with me bathing and dressing their "babies."

Red-Plate Special

We have a special custom called the red-plate special. We have a red cloth napkin, napkin ring, placemat, and glass. Whoever has been honored for something that day (talk in church, honor report card, kind deed), gets served dinner on the red place setting. Even Mom and Dad are included. Everyone loves it!

Personalized Tablecloth

As each child grows old enough to cook meals, we aid him in selecting material for his personalized tablecloth. He draws in pencil any animal, object, scene, or words he desires, in addition to his name and the date. Liquid embroidery is then used to create a lasting tablecloth, which is used whenever it's his turn to cook.

Love Cards

My mother cuts words and pictures out of magazines to make unique birthday and love cards for her grandchildren.

Handprints in Kitchen

Cookie jars and napkin holders can be made using children's handprints. Use a jigsaw to cut around the imprint of a child's hand on two pieces of wood. Add a bottom strip between the two, and a unique napkin holder is formed. A cookie jar with the handprints of each child glazed on the outside is a special way to remember children.

Fragrance on Linens

When I make my teenage girls' beds I sprinkle powder or spray a little cologne on their linens. They love it.

Surprises

My family members never know what to expect when they reach into pockets, move their pillows, or look on their bedroom doors. A stick of gum, a candy bar, or a poem listing their good qualities may be found.

Lunch Box Love

I'll often put a little "I love you" note in my husband's or children's lunch boxes. Sometimes it's in the form of a cartoon.

Badge of Love

One morning I awarded my children badges to wear as they left for school. Each badge was a star made from cardboard covered with aluminum foil. A safety pin on the back fastened it to their clothes. I told them to wear their badges all day as a reminder of my love for them. They were to count how many people asked why they wore them. When they returned home, I would give them a nickel for each inquiry. When asked, their answer was to be, "It's a badge of importance," but it was really a reminder of my love for them.

A Key to the House

All of my older children have their own house keys, which they wear around their necks or in pockets or purse, depending on age. The neighbor also has a key so that my children will always have the security and sense of importance of being able to gain entrance into the house. Little ones anticipate the time they can have their own key, which is when they go to school.

Handmade Gift

A child feels important and loved when he receives a personalized handmade gift, such as a bedspread quilt I made for my son. I sent squares to each of his relatives, asking them to embroider their names (such as Cousin Tami) plus pictures pertaining to my son (football player). Coloring book pictures trace well and can be used as stencils.

Treasured Possession

When my mother presented me with a crazy quilt compiled of squares of material from my old dresses, I felt her love deeply. I treasure that quilt now because I'm able to reminisce about the times I wore each of those dresses.

Good Guy Pillowcase

A pillowcase embroidered with a picture of a child with a halo is given to reward good behavior. The "good guy" gets to use it overnight. To avoid competition, I have more than one good guy pillowcase.

A Dime for Reliance
I tuck a dime away in my child's desk at school, a pocket, or a purse to help him feel secure and self-reliant. My youngsters never leave without a dime to call home in case of emergencies.

Books of Life
After years of accumulating treasures and pictures for each of my children I finally decided I had to make those long-awaited books. I wanted them to be special and meaningful so I decided to take several months making them without feeling rushed. I planned to give them as Christmas presents. These are some of the things I included:

1. A separate section for each year of life. At the beginning of each section I wrote a preface page describing them, their friends, the family, and any incidents I could recall pertaining to that particular year.

2. A summary of popular movies, TV shows, tunes, as well as pictures of the "in" fashions of the year.

3. A letter describing my love and hopes for them, who I thought they were and could become, and all the important counsel I had in my heart for them.

4. Letters from their father and grandparents that included all the cute memories they recalled about each child.

5. Pictures, mementos, and squares of materials from favorite blankets, shirts, or dresses.

These books were the last gifts to be opened Christmas morning. The children were truly touched by the love and thought that went into each book. They spent the rest of Christmas day reading, remembering, and sharing thoughts with one another. My reward was great. Now I try to help them keep the books current.

FAMILY TRADITIONS

"Families should establish traditions that are uniquely theirs, and parents should be alert to situations that may be used to establish traditions. Children can be encouraged at family council meetings to express ideas for traditions. All ideas may not be used, but if a family plans how to use some of the ideas, some traditions will develop. Families who have done this have found great satisfaction and have strengthened and solidified their family." (*Relief Society Courses of Study,* 1978-79, p. 87.)

CHRISTMAS

Temple Visit
During Christmas season we always visit the temple grounds as a family. This has become a very sacred part of our Christmas celebration.

Christmas Yule Log
Each year we have a Christmas yule log. A big red bow, nuts, and pine cones attached with hot wax decorate our log, which we burn during a fireside before bedtime on Christmas Eve. We listen to the story of Christ's birth as the log burns.

Handmade Exchange
On Christmas Eve Mom and Dad give each family member a handmade gift. The children are encouraged to do the same as they get old enough.

Gifts for Needy
Each year instead of exchanging gifts the adult members of my family pool that money to use for a needy person. Last year my widowed sister-in-law received the much-needed help.

Wrapped with Art
My mother looks forward to her Christmas packages because I wrap them with my children's artwork. The children are pleased, and I don't have the problem of throwing old pictures out.

Five More Days

To take the tension out of Christmas we put goodies in stockings from December 20 to the 24. Such things as toothpaste, small games, and pencil and paper may be given.

Ornaments for Each

I let each child purchase one new ornament for our Christmas tree each year. They are stored in separate boxes, marked with the child's name. He places his ornament on the tree when we decorate. These ornaments will go with the children as they marry.

Sleep in One Room

Our eight children have created their own tradition of all sleeping in the oldest child's room on Christmas Eve. They talk, sing, and anticipate the next day late into the evening. It is a time of excitement and closeness for them.

Thank You Party

A few days after Christmas, when the newness of toys wears off and boredom sets in, we hold a thank-you party. I provide thank-you cards, stamps, pens, and a treat. We all sit down and talk over the gifts we received, then write out thanks to the givers.

Gift of Love

On Christmas Eve, each member of our family is given as many small cards as there are people in our family. On these cards everyone writes a "gift of love" for each family member. The rules are that the gift has to be a gift of the self. It can't cost anything and can be used at any time during the next year. Example: "I will do your dishes one time." "I will get the kids ready for bed for one full week."

Family Fireside

On Christmas Eve, after reading
the story of the first Christmas,
our family gathers in a
semicircle around the fireplace,
and each member bears his
testimony.

Ribbons with Gifts

We have a special dinner for our
family on Christmas Eve. I
always tie red ribbons to the
light fixture above our table
(one for each member). A ribbon
floats down to each place setting
and is attached to a special
small gift.

Santa's Snack

Santa always looks forward to a
snack of cookies and milk when
he arrives in our home. A note
saying "thank you" is placed for
him near the plate. Each child
signs this note before going to
bed. In the morning they find
one half-eaten cookie on the
plate and a sleigh bell as
evidence of his visit.

Secret Pals

On December first we draw for
secret pals within the family
and do good deeds for those
whose names we draw. We
change pals once each week
until Christmas.

Paper Chain Links

I make twenty-five chain links
and hang them both sides of my
December calendar. The
children take off one link each
night before going to bed.

Traditional Nightgowns

Each year for as long as I can
remember my mother has made
nightgowns for all her daughters
and granddaughters for
Christmas Eve opening. The
number was up to fifteen this
year but there they were,
anticipated and enjoyed.

Burn the Days

Our favorite tradition began a long time ago when the girls started to ask, "How many days before Christmas?" We bought a white candle and pasted the numbers twelve down to one on it. Each night, during supper, we would burn one number off.

Christmas Pageant

Each Christmas Eve the children in our family act out the Christmas story as it is being read from the Bible. I have a box containing old bathrobes, pieces of colorful taffeta, terry towels, white gauze, and material for Mary's dress. There is much fun and excitement as the children create their own costumes.

We have found this tradition to be an excellent missionary tool when we invite our neighbors to join us. Their children participate and look forward to it each year. Variation: For a family gathering with many young girls wanting to be Mary, serve a dessert with one almond, and the girl with the nut gets to be Mary.

Pick Your Cookie

Our Christmas tree has gingerbread boys and girls on it decorated with the neighborhood children's names. Just before Christmas we invite them to "pick their cookie."

For the Neighbors

On Christmas Eve we always take a plate of goodies to the neighbors. After singing to them we return home to decorate a gingerbread sleigh or cookies.

Family Talent

After a big Christmas dinner with all our relatives, every member performs in a family program. Any talent, such as tumbling, singing, or reading poetry, is shared.

Good Deed Straws

From December first on we have a manger and a straw pile. Each time any of us see or do a good deed we put a straw into the manger. On Christmas Eve, when we reenact the nativity scene, we place a doll on the manger filled with straw "good deeds."

Christmas in Other Lands

Each family home evening throughout the month of December, we feature a new foreign country. We explore its Christmas traditions and customs, read a Christmas story either about or from that country, and serve the country's traditional Christmas dessert for refreshments.

Festive Pancakes

At least one morning in December our family could always count on being served green pancakes with strawberry syrup, topped with whipped cream. Mom never told us just when it would be, but it always happened, and we watched and waited for it.

VALENTINE'S DAY

Heart Biscuits
I include baking powder biscuits in my Valentine's Day menu— cut with a heart-shaped cutter.

Almond in the Cake
I prepare a heart-shaped cake with one almond or raisin dropped in the batter. Whoever gets this in his piece gets to stay up half an hour later than usual that night.

Valentine Collection
Several years ago I started buying my daughter something small and special for each Valentine's Day. Now she calls it her Valentine's collection. I have added such items as little porcelain figures, small decorated boxes, a charm for her bracelet, and a tiny mirror with porcelain hearts.

Love Notes
The week preceding Valentine's Day I have for the centerpiece of our table a nicely decorated, heart-shaped box with flowers around it. There is a slit in the top of the box and, to the side, a pencil and small note pad. "Love notes" are written and deposited in the box throughout the week by family members, and before eating our Valentine's Day dinner we read them.

Red and White
Valentine's Day dinner is always very special, served on our best china. We always have something red and white for dessert.

Valentine's Day Favor

I cut paper towel tubes into lengths of about four inches, fill with goodies, and wrap in white tissue paper and red ribbons to be placed on the plate of each family member for dinner on Valentine's Day.

Red Rose

On Valentine's morning each of my girls can always look forward to finding a single red rose in her bedroom with a note of appreciation for her sweetness and beauty.

Red Balloons

I blow up red balloons (without tying knots) and write messages of love on the outside, round and round, with black Magic Marker. I deflate the balloons and use them as favors on place cards for Valentine's dinner.

Giant Valentine

We have a special tradition of selecting one lonely person, making a giant original Valentine for him, and delivering it personally on Valentine's Day.

Cookies

On Valentine's Day we bake, decorate, and deliver heart-shaped cookies for our special friends.

Love across the Miles

The week or two before Valentine's Day I decorate a shoebox and fill it with paper, pencils, and stamped envelopes. It is set out where all can use it. I encourage the children to write one love or thank-you note a day to relatives we haven't seen in a while.

EASTER

New Beginnings
New clothes and shoes were always something to look forward to at Easter time when I was a girl. Now I provide the same for my children, but I make a point of explaining that the new clothes are a symbol of all that Easter means: new life, hope of a new beginning, casting off the old and worn out and starting again fresh and clean. I explain how this relates to the resurrection of Christ.

Symbolism of Egg
While coloring and decorating our Easter eggs we talk of why the egg is the symbol of Easter.

Onion Skin Colors
For a change, try coloring Easter eggs by using onion skins. Boil these along with the eggs. The eggshells come out different, interesting colors, maroon to light orange.

Clay Baskets
Our family makes small braided Easter baskets out of salt clay. We fill them with grass and tiny eggs and deliver them to home teaching families.

Saturday Bunny
In our family, the Easter bunny comes the night before Easter so that we can keep the Sabbath holy. He usually brings quiet toys that could be used in church.

Shared Sunrise

Each Easter morning our family rides out to a park with a lovely view to watch the sunrise. We talk of our blessings and the meaning of Easter, then return to a breakfast of Easter breads and juice.

Symbolic Breads

Each year on the Saturday before Easter my daughters and I make Easter breads. Many books are available with step-by-step instructions. These breads are not only beautiful to look at and delicious to eat, but most are symbolic and provide an opportunity to discuss the meaning of Easter.

Egg Throw

At our Easter picnic, held on Saturday, we always have a raw-egg-throwing contest. Each person stands facing a partner and tosses an egg to him. For each successful catch the partners step back another step until the egg breaks en route. The couple with the last unbroken egg wins.

Easter Story

One year it dawned on us that we always read the Christmas story on the eve of Christmas, but what of the Easter story? Since then we have made a point of reading the Easter story together as a family each year before Easter dinner.

THANKSGIVING

Count Your Blessings
Everyone writes a list of blessings for which they are thankful. Before dinner a prize is given to the one with the longest list.

Sharing Dinner
We invite at least one lonesome person to share our Thanksgiving dinner.

Fresh Butter
Our children make fresh butter for Thanksgiving dinner. They mold it for the table setting.

Indian Cookie
A Thanksgiving treat is made out of a round gingerbread cookie. Decorated with icing, an Indian's face complete with feather can be created.

Family Portrait
Thanksgiving is the perfect day to have the family picture taken. Everyone is together, and there is always an extra person to click the shutter. I use this picture to give to relatives and also to use on our Christmas cards.

110

Leaves at the Door

We live in a city so we go out to the country and gather autumn leaves to be scattered at the front door on Thanksgiving. It's a cozy way to greet guests.

Blessings Shared

We begin each Thanksgiving dinner with seven kernels of corn on each plate. Each person shares a blessing for each kernel.

Hidden Fortunes

We always have a large bowl of walnuts for cracking. Among them are some special ones; I crack them open, remove the meat, and insert Thanksgiving day fortunes. Then I glue the shells back together.

BIRTHDAY

Grandma Aprons
We have started a tradition of making aprons every two years for each of our grandparents on their birthdays. The aprons are made of navy blue material with white pockets all along the bottom. Each child is given a piece of white paper the exact size of a pocket. He can color any picture he wants for his grandparents with fabric crayons, and he must sign his art work with his signature. The pictures transfer with an iron onto the pockets and become a permanent record of love. My mother wears hers to work and whenever guests are over.

Mailbox Balloons
To help birthday party guests find their way to our home, we always fasten colorful balloons to our mailbox.

Birthday Bulletin Board
I prepare a bulletin board in a very special way for each of the children's birthdays. The board is covered with birthday wrapping paper for the background. I put up pictures of each year of the child's life, certificates of baptism, blessing, and birth, and any special accomplishments. This hangs for one week.

Wrapping Paper Lining
After each child's birthday, I use his discarded wrapping paper as drawer lining in his dresser. It not only gives me an excuse to sort outgrown clothes, but it acts as a reminder all year of his last birthday party.

Money Cake

A tradition that has now been passed to the third generation is to have a money cake for each birthday (especially loved by children six to twelve years old). Pennies, nickels, dimes and quarters are boiled until sterile and dropped into batter of a layer cake. There is great excitement as the cake is cut and eaten.

Collage

My children enjoy art projects, so I encourage each to cut and glue his birthday cards into a collage. It hangs decoratively on his bedroom wall until the next year.

Accomplishments

A special letter of tribute listing the year's accomplishments and unusual experiences is given to each member of our family on his birthday. It is then added to his book of remembrance.

Candle Holders

Lifesaver candies work well as birthday candle holders.

Goals

Goals are written and sealed in an envelope by each family member on his birthday. They will be opened and discussed in a private interview with Dad on the following birthday.

Journal

On their twelfth birthdays our children receive journals, with the responsibility of keeping them themselves.

Blowup Invitation

Birthday invitations written on a balloon with Magic Marker and then deflated are a favorite at our house.

In the Dark

We wait until after dark to light candles on the birthday cake. The lights are turned out as "Happy Birthday" is sung. The candles are then blown out.

His Special Day

Each birthday person may choose what he wants for breakfast and dinner on his special day. His wishes are honored and we have had many surprises, especially for breakfast, from strawberry waffles with whipped cream to simple Cream of Wheat. The birthday child also is relieved of any household responsibilities for the day.

Tribute

Before the evening meal on someone's birthday, everyone takes a turn paying tribute to the honored one.

In the Bag

Putting refreshments in small paper bags for small children's parties is a time saver and also prevents a mess.

NEW ARRIVAL

Baby Bank Account
An individual bank account teaches a child to save and gives him a sense of importance. At birth a sum equal to his weight (8 lbs. 6 ozs.) could be deposited in the bank ($8.06). One dollar for each year could be added on birthdays. Perhaps one dollar could be added for special achievements as he grows up. When a boy is ready for his mission, a nice sum of money will have accumulated.

His Color
The day we bring a new baby home from the hospital, all the family gathers together to determine collectively what color is most suited for him. He then retains his color throughout his life for personal items such as Christmas stockings, sheets, and gift wrapping.

Blessing Dress
Before our first child was born I made a beautiful "blessing dress." I spent time making it very perfect knowing that each of our children would be blessed in it. It has now been used six times. I hope many grandchildren will also use it.

8 lbs. 14 oz. Turkey
Whenever a baby is born to someone we especially like, our family buys their family a turkey the same size as the baby's birth weight. We have it ready when the new mother gets home from the hospital.

Birthday Newspaper
Whenever I have a new baby, I save the day's newspaper so that when he is grown he will have a record of what happened on the day he was born.

SPIRITUAL

Temple Greeting
We are fortunate enough to live close to a temple. When someone in our family gets married, the cousins and young relatives wait inside the visitors center until the new bride and groom come out of the temple.

Father's Blessing
Before school begins each year, my husband gives each child a father's blessing. He tells them what is expected of them. Being guided by the Spirit, he points out special positive qualities about each. He also doesn't forget the preschoolers. They enjoy this special time and grow to look forward to and expect it.

Special Day
When there is a baptism in our house, the child is encouraged to fast before, and then the whole family goes out to a restaurant for dinner afterward.

Book of Remembrance
In our family, a book of remembrance is given to each child at his baptism.

Family Fast
Our family fasts together on a day other than fast Sunday for solutions to problems or out of gratitude. Little ones are asked merely to give something up.

Picture of Prophet
We always have a picture of the current prophet hanging in the house in a prominent place where all can see it.

GENERAL

Thumbtack Messages

We have our own family system of leaving messages. Instead of leaving a note on the door we use colored thumbtacks. Everyone knows red means "I'll be right back," blue means "I'll be back by dinner," and so on.

Harvest Dinner

When our summer garden has grown enough we go out and pick our vegetables and have a "harvest dinner." We serve only what we have grown, along with homemade bread. Our children love this and look forward to it.

Snuggling

Our family snuggles together to hear continued stories in which one of us starts making up a story and then stops at a critical point where another picks the tale up, and so on until someone finishes it.

Gourmet Night

Because the cost of dining out has become prohibitive, we now have a "restaurant at home" night once a month. I provide a menu, complete with fancy dessert, the morning before so the family can anticipate what I will serve. Usually I will try something new. I provide a lovely centerpiece, place cards, and soft music. We turn the lights down and use candles. Each member must dress up for dinner and use his best manners.

Note Left Behind

When we leave each other for vacations or business trips, the ones left behind can always find little notes or treats in locations they're certain to see, such as under pillows, near toothbrushes, and in the toy box.

Family Flags

We have family flags. Each child designs his own flag in crayon, paint, or stitchery. I frame and hang them in a grouping in the family room. We plan to copy and paint them on our mailbox.

New Convert

Homemade bread or other goodies are made and delivered to each new convert in our ward.

Sharing

Once a month we invite a widow to join us for a meal or family outing.

For the Bride

My mother-in-law does something special for each of her new daughters-in-law. As soon as they are married she presents each of them with two little booklets, one containing names and addresses of all her husband's closest friends and relatives, and another with recipes of all her husband's favorite foods.

Visit the Sick

I teach my children to serve others by taking them each week to visit elderly people at nursing homes. The children sing songs, teach the patients crafts, or just listen to them reminisce.

Unbirthday

Several times during the year we have an unbirthday or nonholiday (turkey and all the trimmings) for our evening meal.

House Party

Every year on the anniversary of the day we moved into our home we give our house a birthday party. We get it nice and clean, fix anything broken, and buy something special to help make and keep it lovely.

Reading

I read a chapter a day to my children from a chosen book. This is a tradition I brought from my own childhood.

ORGANIZATION

"For all of us there are twenty-four hours in a day. Each day is measured out in the same proportion to everyone. What shall we do with this priceless possession? Each of us must make our own decision, depending on our love, our willingness to serve, and our determination and ambition." (*Children's Friend,* May 1954, p. 204.)

SETTING PRIORITIES

List of Importance
I find that having a priority list of the things I want to accomplish each day is a necessity in avoiding confusion. The list is made either mentally or on paper during my prayer and meditation time. Because I have much to do, I have to number each item according to importance and do them in that order. Most of the time I don't finish the list because of unexpected interruption, but I anticipate and accept these disturbances as challenges. Included on the list is time for myself and our children.

Stay Home
I reserve one day a week for solely "being a mother." I'll not go anywhere on this day. No doctor appointments or visitors to our home are planned.

Relax Pressure
When I realized my husband thought the house was clean when it was merely picked up, I realized I could relax the pressure on myself if vacuuming and dusting were not always done. Now I set my goal to have the house surface tidy—all beds made, bathrooms and kitchen sinks clean, and clutter removed. I do these chores first (planning another quick picking up of clutter before Dad returns); then I do those things that are most important to me, such as cleaning the refrigerator.

Weekly Schedule

I divide my housework into a weekly schedule for myself. I do a little each day so that by Saturday I don't have quite as much work to do.

Pamper Self

I arise at least an hour before anyone else so that my personal "pampering," such as prayers, scripture reading, exercising, and grooming, is completed before others appear. After my shower, the laundry is started and going while I groom. I make my own bed and start breakfast so that when the children awaken I am ready for them.

Hate Housework

Some days I can't bear the thought of doing housework, so I read one chapter of a good book. Then I clean one room, go back to my book for another chapter, and so on. By the end of the day I feel as though I've lazed around all day, but my household duties are done. I can't always do this because of outside activities, but it really works when possible.

More Hours

I have eliminated watching television from my schedule. The result is more hours to pursue my own interests. I don't even know what I'm missing anymore and I don't care!

Help

Because my children are little, I hire two high school girls to help me once a week. One girl takes my preschoolers to the park while the other helps me clean the house. For my serenity, it's worth the financial sacrifice.

Goodnight Clean House

My husband and I instituted this rule several years ago: Before we go to bed he and I always toss clutter into a plastic basket. It has to be put away by the children in the morning, but I always wake up to an uncluttered house.

Complete Job

I find that cleaning one room at a time works for me because I have the feeling of completing the job after each room.

Don't Get Behind

I try not to get behind in my work or I'll spend the next day trying to catch up.

SAVING TIME

Night Work
Occasionally I'll have extra energy at night. It's surprising how quickly the refrigerator can be cleaned or floors mopped when no one else is around. The next day I have more time for other interests.

Learn and Work
I listen to Book of Mormon tapes while I do my housework. My thoughts are then on the scriptures and I'm learning.

Junk Drawer
To save steps I have a junk drawer both upstairs and downstairs containing such items as scissors, tape, rulers, thread, and needles.

Pockets
I wear an apron with pockets while I clean. Any misplaced items are popped into the pockets.

Cleaning Box
A plastic open box with a handle stores such items as rags, bottles of cleaners, and brushes. When I clean, I carry it with me from room to room.

Overlap Chores
I can accomplish a lot in a small amount of time if I overlap chores. If the phone connections are well placed, I can iron, clean counters, stove, and cupboards, or fold clothes while talking on the phone. A chicken can be cooking while the floors are being scrubbed and a load of clothes is being washed.

Going Upstairs

Saving steps is important to me, so when I have items to take upstairs, I place them by the stairs to be carried up when I have to make trips anyway.

Beat the Clock

I set a timer for myself so I'll finish a chore quickly. Beating the clock becomes a game; if I beat it, I feel great!

Cook without Steps

My kitchen is planned so that I can stand in one spot to cook. Within my reach below are pots, pans, and bowls. In front of me is the silverware drawer and above is the spice shelf. A built-in chopping board is on the counter, while the range is to the left. The refrigerator and sink are behind me two steps away.

Cleaning Aids

I keep cleaning items in the bathroom, kitchen, and laundry room in order to save steps.

Personalized Colors

I've saved hours of time by assigning each person his own color for items such as towels, cups, toothbrushes, washcloths, and anything else that requires constant cleaning or laundering.

Errands

When I have errands to run that I know will be burdensome with my six- to twelve-year-olds, I drop them off at the library and pick them up on my way back home. The older ones are responsible for the younger.

No Wasted Time

I seem to do a lot of chauffeuring for my five active children. I try to plan to do my grocery shopping and other errands while they're busy with lessons or practices, but sometimes I have time to spare. A notepaper pad or fingernail polish and file fill in those spare moments profitably.

On Hand Supply

If I find an appropriate toy or other article on sale, I will buy it for a future birthday party present. My children are always asked to parties, sometimes at the last minute, and this supply saves me time, effort, and money.

Handy Gift Wrap

After searching for suitable wrapping paper at the last minute, I finally used newspaper to wrap a gift. Tied with a colorful ribbon, it looked quite clever.

CUPBOARDS, CLOSETS, AND DRAWERS

Junk Box

My cupboards and closets seemed orderly after I donated items I hadn't used for a year to the church garage sale. I keep a "questionable junk" box available in the garage for items I never use but can't yet give away.

Turntables

Round turntables hold my spices, condiments, soaps, medicines, and makeup for easy access in my cupboards.

Low Closet Rods

My husband installed closet rods low enough so that little children can reach to hang up their own clothes.

Little Boxes

Little boxes of different sizes keep my kitchen drawers orderly. Both the lids and bottoms can be used to hold items.

A Door? Shut It!

Closets are never orderly in my house because spending time with my children is more important to me. Instead of feeling guilty, I have a philosophy that if something has a door, you should just shut it and forget about it until there is time to clean it.

Egg Carton

An empty egg carton is a magic storage bin for socks in my preschooler's drawers.

Hooks for Coats
My children have hooks for their coats hanging on the inside door of the hall closet. They are low enough for easy access.

More Room
I have much more room in dresser drawers now that sweaters are stored in sweater boxes on closet shelves.

Clothes Placement
Pictures of articles of clothing taped to the inside of drawers illustrate for my little ones where each item belongs. They no longer mix the socks with the shirts when they see where to put their clean clothes.

Wooden Cartons
Closet space has doubled because I stack wooden soda or milk cases on the floor against the back wall of the closet. Separate compartments conveniently hold items such as toys or shoes. These cartons also make decorative knickknack cupboards when hung on the wall.

Outgrown Items
I used to hate cleaning children's closets and drawers because I would collect too many individual cardboard boxes full of outgrown clothes. The rooms were clean but the garage was cluttered with boxes. My problem was solved once I discovered plastic trash cans with lids. Each holds a large volume of clothes, sorted according to size within plastic bags.

Snap Hooks
Snap hooks designed to hold brooms are convenient in children's closets to hold baseball bats and toy guns.

TOYS

Rotate
I rotate toys by storing half in boxes in garage rafters. After a few months, I will bring those toys to the toy box and take the others to the garage, and so on. The children are delighted with their forgotten toys, and I don't have a storage problem or unnecessary clutter.

Toy Closet
Clear plastic shoe or sweater boxes have solved my toy storage problems. All the parts to one toy (such as a View Master with reels) go into one box, all balls in another, and so forth. One of my linen closets has become a toy closet, so the see-through boxes sit on the shelves for easy identification. I control what goes in and out of the closet when preschoolers play. One toy must be replaced before another is selected.

Tiny Toys
I save potato chip, powdered drink, or beef jerky cans with lids for storing little toys. Great for buttons, bobbypins, and crayons too!

Shoe Bag
My children have shoe bags hanging on the inside of their bedroom doors. One pocket is for balls, another for cars, ribbons, or other small items.

Wall Storage
Velcro strips stapled to a bedroom wall and sewn or glued onto toys such as stuffed animals allow those lightweight toys to be stored on the wall.

No Scattering

I discovered that when all the toys are in one room, I can control the toy scattering. I move the toy box into the front room in the morning. Before Dad comes home the children and I pick up the toys and move the box to a back bedroom. No more toys scattered through the house.

Baby's Toys

Snap-on curtain rings hold toys in crib, high chair, or playpen. Toys for older children can be snapped onto these rings and hung on hooks for storage.

Puzzle Pieces

I find that pieces of puzzles would be scattered if I didn't tape plastic wrap around the completed puzzle. The pictures can be seen but the pieces can't fall out while stored. When the child wishes to use the puzzle, the tape is removed so that the wrap can be replaced later.

Coded Puzzles

After trying to sort out mixed puzzle pieces, I color coded the back of each piece with a dot of fingernail polish. All the red dots belong to one puzzle, the pink ones to another.

Game Boards

I covered game boards, such as those that come with checkers or chess, with shellac to preserve them.

Color Coding Records

Little children who don't read have trouble matching correct records to corresponding folders. By color coding the record with a colored dot, a child can match it to the correct cover by searching for a corresponding color.

KITCHEN WORK

Weekly Menu
Once a week I make a weekly menu. It helps budget time and money; I'm also able to make certain my family has a variety of nutritious meals. Once I have the menu planned, I write down the grocery list, and on Friday the shopping is done.

Enjoy Afternoon Lag
I try to bake and prepare meals in the morning while I'm fresh so that the afternoon lag can be spent in rest or quiet work. A crock-pot left cooking lifts the mealtime morale when I'm gone all day.

Freeze Ahead
I prepare double portions when fixing a meal. One half is used that evening, the other half is frozen for use next week, on the Sabbath, or to share with the ill.

No Mess at Noon
I have to straighten the kitchen only in the morning and evening, because I fix everyone's lunches, including my own, in the morning or late evening. Preschoolers enjoy their own sack lunches, especially when we have an outdoor picnic.

Piggyback Entertaining
When we are ready to entertain, my husband and I always plan for guests for two consecutive nights. We use the same menu, so I only do major cooking once, the house is already clean, and the centerpiece does double duty.

Think Ahead

On Monday mornings, I will have sandwich makings available for the children to make their own sandwiches for the week. They merely select their sandwiches from the freezer the rest of the week.

Cupcakes

An ice cream scoop is a useful tool for filling cupcake papers without a mess.

Quick Cleanup

Each family member is expected to carry his own dirty place setting to the sink as well as to put one other item away after each meal. The table is cleared effortlessly and time is saved.

PAPERWORK

Message Center
I created a work space and message center with a desk and bulletin board in my kitchen. No more scattered paperwork!

Throw It Out!
I throw away any mail I don't want the day it arrives, before it accumulates in unsightly piles to be sorted later.

Babysitter's Guide
Placed near my phone is a babysitter's folder containing a list of phone numbers, including those of the doctor, home teachers, and police and fire departments. Also included is an emergency hospital release signed by my husband and me in case of needed medical assistance.

Never Forget Birthdays
In January I place birthday cards with addressed and stamped but not sealed envelopes in a birthday book listed according to month. Each fast Sunday I check the book, include personal notes, and seal and mail the month's envelopes. It takes time in January to organize, but I never forget a birthday!

Paper Clutter in Box
A box with a slit on the lid sits on my counter to catch coupons, new recipes, and other papers until I have time to sort them. I decorated it with leftover scraps of kitchen wallpaper.

Paying Bills

If I pay bills as they arrive instead of waiting until they pile up, the job is not so cumbersome and overwhelming.

File Schoolwork

Because I have four "school-agers," school papers would pile up if I didn't require each child to file his own work after I see it. He may discard whatever he wishes, but his special work hangs on the kitchen wall for a time. I purchased several large folders at the post office (cheaper than at the store) and placed them in boxes labeled with each child's name. When his box is full of completed folders, the child sorts them again to discard unwanted work. The entire box is then placed in the garage rafters for storage. Note: Cardboard tubes from waxed paper or aluminum foil are also handy for storing artwork.

Children's Artwork

I write letters to close friends and relatives on the back of my children's artwork.

Records on Calendar

It's easier for me to jot daily episodes on a calendar each day than it is to write lengthy letters, so I'll just drop the calendar in the mail at the end of the month to my son on a mission or child away at school. It may also be placed in my journal if I haven't had time to record in it.

Copies for Journal

Whenever I write letters to personal friends or relatives, I make a carbon copy to be placed in my journal. Sometimes I'll photocopy pages out of my journal to send as letters to those dear to me.

Carry Notebook

I always carry a notebook in my purse to record inspirational thoughts, ideas for baby books, letters to friends, and grocery lists in case I find myself wasting time in such places as doctor's offices, bus stops, or stalled traffic.

HELPING HANDS

Grumbling No More
If a child complains about doing a certain chore, I add another to his list. I keep adding for each complaint until he learns to be quiet. I must remember to make certain the extra chore is completed or else he won't believe me the next time. One time my daughter added seven extra chores before she stopped complaining. I was firm in her punishment even though it hurt me, but she doesn't grumble anymore.

Everyone Works
In our house, work is distributed fairly among all family members. The children are trained to do a job as well as I do. It takes supervising time, but it pays off eventually. Seven- and eight-year-olds can clean a bathroom, especially if spray cleaner is used. Two- and three-year-olds can certainly pick up mislaid articles.

Child Is Boss
Saturday we spend working as a family. Occasionally we allow one child to be the boss. He may assign anyone, including Mom and Dad, reasonable jobs. The goal is to get the house sparkling clean and everyone involved, including the boss, even if it's only to guide little ones in their chores.

Draw for Jobs
We change chores weekly during family home evening. We either draw chores from a hat or pass them from one to another. If the children draw from a hat, I sometimes slip a "free" paper in so someone feels rewarded by not having a weekly chore. Each still has daily chores, such as keeping his own room clean.

Litterbug Pillowcase
Any misplaced item belonging to a family member is placed in a litterbug pillowcase, which has an unhappy bug drawn on it in fabric crayon. If a child wants an item back, he must pay for it or do a chore. Each week I show them the articles, saying that in one month they will be donated to the needy if not retrieved. I don't nag anymore, and the house is uncluttered. Note: When this rule applies to Mom and Dad too, the children enjoy it more.

Grocery Bags
Everyone in the family is expected to help bring in at least one grocery bag when I return from shopping. If I have help unloading and putting away goods, they have a happy mother. If someone fails to help, his bag of unperishables sits in the car. He will not get to eat his next meal until his bag is in.

INCENTIVES

Teamwork
Our family sometimes will divide into teams to see which group finishes its chores first. The work must pass inspection. The winning team is treated to ice cream cones by the losing team. One time the losers had to do one chore for the winners during the week.

Mother's Gift Bag
During family home evening we have a mother's gift bag. If all his chores have been completed for the week, a child gets to draw out of it. Treats such as granola bars or coupons giving "free" privileges are drawn. The privileges could be anything that's important to them, such as, "This paper means you can be late for dinner one time next week," or "This may be exchanged for a quarter."

Pick-It-Up-As-You-Go-Club
We have a "pick-it-up-as-you-go club" in our house so that when someone uses something, it is put away promptly. Anyone who forgets to pick up his own things stands a chance of losing the club treat, which may be an ice cream sundae.

Clever Titles
Our children enjoy titles for their special jobs. The storage clerk organizes and inventories all food storage. The secretary clips and organizes food coupons for me. The maintenance man hangs pictures and makes repairs.

Music

Singing together while working as a team makes chores seem light. Soft background music also helps set a soothing mood while work is being completed.

Earning Money

A weekly allowance plus extra money for completed chores not on their list is given to our children so they have the opportunity to pay tithing, pay themselves, and save.

Hidden Coupons

I'll hide little notes or coupons worth surprises, such as, "This entitles you to miss a punishment," or "Give this to Mom and she will do one chore for you tomorrow," in places where the work is done.
Whoever does the chore gets the surprise.

Trading Stamps

I give stamps (small stickers or decals) for each job completed. The children have books made of old calendar pages cut down and stapled together. With full books they are able to buy surprises, which I have collected from garage sales.

TINY HELPING HANDS

Step by Step
When the children are little, I have to instruct them step by step how to do a job. I continually aid and inspect their work until it becomes easy for them. Then my time is more free.

Diaper Man
Our next-to-youngest child is in charge of taking wet diapers from the changing table to the diaper pail. We just call our "diaper man" and she comes running to do her job. Each child has had a chance to do that job, and they love it.

Supervisors
I'll assign one older child to supervise a younger one in his job so that I'm free to assist on a floating basis.

Set the Table
In order to teach the children how to set the table, I have a pattern drawn on the back of a place mat. They are to follow it to see where to place the knives, forks, and spoons.

Games
I always try to make each job as much of a game as possible. For example, when picking up blocks, I may help my little ones "make baskets" by throwing the blocks gently into the block box.

Not Tall Enough
I keep a stool in the bathroom and one at the kitchen counter for my small child's convenience.

Chores for Tiny Tots
I never underestimate the ability of my little ones. There are many chores they can accomplish if given the chance and proper guidance. I've found the following suitable for preschoolers:
—Scrub walls sprayed by Mom
—Sweep kitchen floor with
    whisk broom and dustpan
—Carry clean laundry to dresser
—Clear kitchen table
—Pick up toys
—Scrub counters

Reward for Remembering
Any time my little ones do a chore without being told I will give them a penny. Brushing teeth, saying prayers, and picking up toys are included.

Dusting Fun
I'll draw faces on old socks used for dusting so the children can play games while working.

WORK CHARTS

Magnetic Bulletin Board
I use a magnetic bulletin board to list daily chores. A covering of contact paper turns a metal cookie sheet into my bulletin board. I use magnets to hold work lists; my favorites are magnetic hooks.

Pockets
Our work list is hanging in the kitchen. I glue open envelopes to a poster board forming two pockets for each child. One pocket is labeled "Work to Be Done," the other, "Work Completed." Each morning I will place work assignments, typed on reusable slips of paper, in the "Work to Be Done" pockets. When chores are done the children place the slips into the other pockets.

Illustrations
Because my little ones are unable to read, I draw or cut pictures from magazines to indicate their chores on the star chart. They are then able to lick and place their own stars. They feel very proud of themselves.

Note on Refrigerator
In the morning I place a note on the refrigerator for each child listing the day's chores. These chores can be done before or after school, but they must be completed before the children can play.

Family Pig

We have a family "pig" made of a piece of flat wood cut into the shape of a pig. Each person's name is painted on the pig, and cup hooks are screwed in opposite the names. Key tags individually marked with chores are hung on the hooks. When the jobs are finished, the tags are placed on the pig's tail.

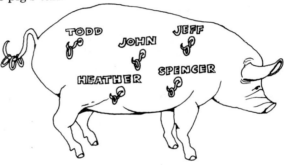

Calendar

We have a daily calendar that the children initial when their work is finished. If I find the work incomplete and the child gone, I'll go get him and make him work the entire afternoon.

Lend a Helping Hand

A poster board titled "Lend a Helping Hand" hangs in our kitchen. I stapled horizontal strips of cardboard on the poster. These strips are labeled with children's names. Slips of paper listing chores are placed inside the "pockets" made by the staples. The children see at a glance what their duties are.

Spin the Circle

I made a circle chart out of cardboard. The inside circle is smaller, with each child's name listed around the edge. It is fastened with a brad in the center to an outer, larger circle, which lists the jobs around the edge. I merely twist the circle to indicate which child will do which chore. Paper clips keep it in place until I change assignments.

Color Codes

Work assignments are color coded in our house: red—clean bathrooms; blue—vacuum; pink—dust. If a child finds a red slip by his name on our chart, he checks the code chart and does the corresponding chore. For variety, I often change the code.

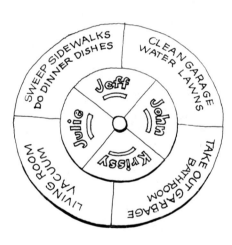

CLEANING SECRETS

Locked Out
We put locks on the outside of older children's rooms so that little ones can't get into "forbidden treasures."

Clean Floors
I do not allow anyone to wear shoes in my house. It's surprising how my rugs and floors stay clean.

Remove Soap Buildup
Kerosene works well to remove soap buildup in showers.

Dust Corners
A soft, medium-sized paintbrush is excellent for dusting those hard-to-get places such as carved wood, ceramics, and corners.

Mildew
Spray window cleaner and a good sturdy brush will remove mildew from bathroom tile. Clorox will also kill mildew.

Dust Quickly
Dusting goes faster when each hand has an old sock on it.

Window Washing
I dry windows after spraying with a commercial spray window cleaner or ammonia by wiping with old newspaper.

Salt Absorbs
I use salt to absorb the mess when a raw egg drops on the floor. A generous amount must be poured on it but it is worth the time and effort saved.

LAUNDRY

Personalized Bins
Boxes, baskets, trays, or dishpans of different colors, one for each family member, can be used for clean laundry. Each child folds and puts his own clothes away. I will fold the clothes for one who is too young, but he must carry his own basket to his room if he can walk.

Mounds of Clothes
I find that if I save the laundry to do once a week, that's all I get accomplished that day (if I can see my way through the mounds). I'm much more organized when I do the laundry continually so it never builds up. I set unfolded clothes near the phone to be folded during the next phone call.

Lost Socks?
We have a supply of safety pins handy to use in pinning each pair of socks together before washing. It saves sorting and folding time and no socks get lost.

Junk Box
We keep a junk box near the washer and dryer. Combs, notes, pencils, or money found in pockets are collected in this box so the owner knows where to find his belongings.

Changing Sheets
I never change all the sheets in one day because the laundry then bogs me down. Instead, I rotate the beds so that everyone has clean sheets once a week. If a child knows it is his day, he will remove his sheets instead of making his bed.

Incentive
To encourage the children to put away their newly washed clothes, which are in their individual baskets, I always put a little treat in the bottom of the basket.

CREATIVE PLAY

A Harvard University study of preschool children found that a child who excels in all areas, both social and academic, has a mother who:
1. Provides lots of objects and toys for the child to play with.
2. Allows freedom to roam and discover.
3. Gives attention to the child when he finds something exciting or when he encounters a problem he can't overcome.
4. Turns everyday situations into enjoyable games.
5. Talks to her child.

BUILDING SELF-ESTEEM

A Place of His Own
I try to have at least one place in each main room in our house for my child to call his own. In the living room it's part of a bookshelf where he can leave his things. In the kitchen it's a low cupboard. In other rooms I have squares of terry towel with loops on the four corners. He can spread these out on the floor and have his own private play area, and if there's not time to put things away the toys can quickly be gathered up by catching up the four corners of the towel and putting it on a hanger to store away till next time.

Makeup Purse
An old purse filled with old, light-colored makeup is a great gift for a little girl.

Look-Alike Doll
I make rag dolls and use yarn the same color as my child's hair (or as close as I can come) to make a doll that looks as much like the child as possible. I make doll clothes out of clothes the child has outgrown or worn out. I also add some of the child's own infant clothes to the doll's wardrobe.

Life-Size Doll
Help your child make a life-size look-alike doll. Lay him down on a piece of butcher paper, trace the outline of his whole body, then give him crayons or paint to fill in the face, hair, and clothes. Let him hang it on the wall or door.

Homemade Rhythm

Providing an outlet with any kind of music is a good way to help a child learn who he is. Rhythm instruments are wonderful to have on hand to use with a piano, with songs on television, and with record player or tape recorder. Here are some ideas you might use:

—Can with lid containing beans or pebbles
—Solid wood block and mallet for pounding
—Box with rubber bands strung across for strumming
—Rubber bands strung across chair for harp
—Pail upside down with sticks for drum
—Washboard and thimbles for fingers
—Kitchen pans and spoons for beating rhythm
—Two pot lids for cymbals
—Cardboard tubes from waxed paper or paper towels for "tooting" through
—Round oatmeal box with wooden sticks
—Inexpensive tambourines
—Baby rattles
—Comb and tissue for humming

Silhouette

Help your child make a silhouette of his profile and mount it on paper.

Enlarged Photo

I have used 8-by-10-inch photographs of my children in several ways:—From a good close-up, spread glue completely over photo and glue to a piece of lightweight cardboard. Trace a simple puzzle on the cardboard side and cut it out. Store in large envelope or small box. — From a full-length photo do as above, except cut only the outline of the child and use as a personal paper doll. Help the child make lots of clothes. These both make wonderful gifts.

Self-Portrait

Provide child with paint equipment or crayons and paper and have him paint a self-portrait. Ask him to tell you about the picture:—What is the child doing? thinking? What does this child like? What doesn't this child like?

The Dress-Up Box

A toy box, an old decorative trunk, a cardboard box, or a large suitcase that can easily slide under a bed are all suitable containers for dress-ups. Contents should include anything that delights your own child. Remember that little boys can have just as much fun dressing up as girls, so be sure to include clothes for him. You may want to include some of the following:

—Crepe paper for hula skirts
—Clean mops for hair
—Old wigs
—Large paper bags
—Old jewelry
—Old hats
—Paper fans
—Feathers
—Old gloves

Making Booklets

Helping a child make various types of booklets is an excellent way of making him feel special. As you put the book together be enthusiastic about the fact that it's his book. Pasting an old or extra photograph of him on the front page makes him feel very important. The booklet can be put together in a number of ways:

—Folding the pages over and tying a string through the center.
—Stapling along the edge.
—Punching holes along edge and tying with colorful yarn.

Booklet titles can be as varied as the child:

—Things they like
—Things they don't like
—Things that are the same color
—Things that are different
—Things that are opposite (big-little, sweet-sour, soft-hard)
—Things that are round, square, or other shapes
—As a child learns to read, an ongoing booklet of words he recognizes from newspapers and magazines
—His own story, recorded by you and illustrated by him.

THE FLANNEL BOARD

Flannel boards can provide hours of creative fun for children. They can be made in a variety of ways and in many different sizes. The figures for placing on the board can also be prepared in numerous ways. Below are some ideas to choose from:

The Board

1. Thin plywood or masonite is suitable for covering.

2. The board can be any size you choose; 20 by 24 inches is a good size.

3. Two pieces of heavy cardboard can be used by joining them together before covering with flannel.

4. Prepared canvas board (available at art supply stores) can be purchased in a wide variety of sizes. This is lightweight yet very sturdy.

The Covering

1. Flannel has been used for years as a covering for the board. There are many new materials on the market now, such as velours, which come in different weights and naps. Shop around and become familiar with what's available before you make your choice. Pay attention to the length of the nap.

2. I make my covering out of a heavyweight velour. Light blue is my choice of colors because it provides a natural sky

background for many of the
figures I use. The long nap on a
good velour makes the figures
"stick" so much easier than the
traditional flannel.

3. I take the measurements
of the board and make the
covering like a tight-fitting
pillowcase, slipping it over the
board and hand stitching it
across the top. This makes it
very easy to undo and launder
as needed. This is also
reversible.

FLANNEL BOARD FIGURES

For Storytelling
I take old storybooks with worn-out covers and adhere iron-on Pellon to the backs of the pictures. The Pellon makes them "rip-proof." If you choose a Pellon weight with some nap on the back the pictures stick without adding flannel, especially to a board covered with velour. I store each story in a separate envelope. Sometimes I tell the children the story, but they also love to tell each other flannel stories.

Contact Paper
Flocked contact paper is easily applied to the back of cut-out figures. It's self-adhesive and easy to use.

Felt Figures
Felt is a natural. Without any backing it sticks to the board with gentle rubbing. In one box I have the following figures for my child to create any number of situations, all from folded felt.
—Simple houses in different colors (holes cut out for windows and doors)
—Trees (green) in different heights
—White clouds
—Strips of green grass
—Colored flowers
—People—many sizes

Sandpaper
Sandpaper can be easily cut and glued to the back of pictures.

Felt Shapes
An envelope filled with different basic shapes (such as squares, rectangles, and circles) helps a child learn to identify and name them.

Alphabet
I have a box containing multicolored felt letters. I include enough of each letter so that as the child develops his skills he can make complete words.

THE TAPE RECORDER

Stories
I tape-recorded children's stories by reading favorite stories into the tape recorder. My children find the tape recorder easier to operate than a record player, so I don't have to help as often.

Favorite Stories
Many times in the evening as I put my child to bed, I will get out the recorder and recapture the day on tape. Each tape contains many days. He would rather listen to this than any story.

Guess the Sound
Try recording different familiar sounds on tape (a door slamming, water running, your voice, Dad's voice, the doorbell). Pause between each sound so that you have time to stop the recorder and let the child identify the sounds as you play the tape for him.

Make More Than One
Whenever I have anything on tape that is precious enough for keeping (such as the child's voice telling stories) I borrow another machine and make duplicates. One I keep in a safe place; the other is available for daily use and enjoyment.

LEARNING THROUGH PLAY

Learning to Pour
Measuring cups, funnels, and different sized containers filled with rice or beans provide entertainment for preschoolers. They enjoy pouring things from one container to another. A little broom and dustpan should also be provided for cleanup.

Balance Beam
We have our own homemade balance beam for our little ones to practice on. My husband simply bought an eight-foot-long-piece of 2 by 4 board and placed it on the floor. As children get older and a little surer of themselves, short pieces of board can be placed under the beam as support to make it a bit more challenging.

Pounding Board
A block of wood, nails, and a hammer keep my son busy for hours. I partially start the nails for him so all he does is pound them down. For preschoolers, a styrofoam block can be substituted for wood.

String the Beads
We make beads out of small salad macaroni. Dye the shells different colors with food coloring and water—just till they absorb the color so they don't get too wet. Spread them on a cookie sheet and dry in the oven at low temperature. Place them in small containers, such as baby food jars, with long shoelaces for stringing.

Open House
I sometimes draw an outline of an open house showing three or four rooms. The children then cut out people and objects from magazines to furnish it.

Homemade Sewing Cards
Children can make their own sewing cards by pasting magazine pictures or artwork to cardboard. Punch holes around edges and provide shoelaces or colorful yarn to thread through holes. You can dip ends of yarn in glue or in nail polish; you can also wrap tape around ends to make them ready to lace. Store in manila envelopes.

Creative Tracing
I cut shapes out of heavy cardboard and let children trace around them to make designs and see how many different things can be made from basic shapes.
—Circles: glasses, sun, ball, wheel, clock
—Rectangle: doors, trucks, tables, newspaper
—Square: windows, house, napkin
—Triangle: trees, boats, tents, mountains, rooftops
  Cookie cutters are also good to use as a basic outline, letting children fill in faces or other details.

READING READINESS

Letters in the Sand
Pour salt or sand in the bottom of a cake pan. Let a child practice his letters by drawing them in the sand. Erase by merely shaking the pan.

Pretzel ABC's
Using small pretzel sticks to form letters is a fun way to help a child learn the ABC's.

Now You See It, Now You Don't
Put many different objects on a tray. Remove them one at a time. Let the child guess which object is gone. Do this until all are gone. Keep the number of items simple enough for success, depending on the age of the child.

Play a Rhyming Game
1. An animal that rhymes with dig?
2. Something to play with that rhymes with wall?
3. An animal that rhymes with log?
4. A vegetable that rhymes with mean?
5. Something white that rhymes with slow?
6. A color that rhymes with mellow?
7. A girl's name that rhymes with hilly?
8. A boy's name that rhymes with airy?
9. Something to sit on that rhymes with air?
10. Something to sleep on that rhymes with Fred?
11. Time of day that rhymes with mine?
12. An animal that rhymes with here?

Refrigerator ABC's

My children play with magnetic letters and numbers on the refrigerator.

Playing School

My children enjoy playing school. One is the teacher, while others are students. A chalkboard, ruler, paper, pencil, old workbooks, and a bell add to the fun. I will join them when I have time, either as a teacher or student.

Read and Do

As my child became able to sound words out, I made her a set of cards containing instructions, such as "close the door," "touch your toe," "come here," and "walk to Dad."

Hand to Back Alphabet

One way I have found to help a child who is just learning the alphabet is to make the letters on his back with my fingers. Everyone loves to have his back scratched, and it helps the child concentrate.

MATCHING AND SORTING

Match the Shapes
Glue a colored piece of construction paper on an 8-by-10-inch piece of cardboard. Cut out different shapes, two at a time. Glue one to the board and keep the other in an envelope for the child to match. You can also do this with numbers to help him identify them.

Card Games
Long before children are old enough to really understand how to play games, Old Maid or Rook cards can be lots of fun. These provide an excellent way to teach the children to categorize and to recognize numbers.

Muffin Tins
On the bottom of the twelve compartments of an egg carton or muffin tin, paint numbers from one to twelve. (For a younger child use half an egg carton or a six-muffin tin.) Give the child exactly 78 pieces of macaroni, pennies, buttons, or round cardboard discs (21 for the smaller container), and have him drop in each numbered compartment a corresponding number of pieces. This game is self-correcting if the correct amount is given initially.

Cracker Matching
Crackers come in all kinds of shapes—circles, rectangles, squares, and even triangles. These can be used for matching and sorting.

Number Games
Old calendars can be cut to provide numbers for number games or merely for recognition.

Nuts and Bolts
In a bottle or covered box I keep twelve different kinds of interesting nuts and bolts. Use egg carton or muffin tin and let child sort till jar is empty.

Jar of Plenty
I keep a jar containing many different objects for sorting. Pennies, white beans, brown beans, large macaroni shells, or small wheel macaroni might be included.

Play Dough Figures
I help my child cut out small, different-shaped objects from play dough. After drying in the oven they are placed in a box for sorting. (Use small round aspirin bottle lids, miniature cookie cutters, etc, for uniformity.)

Match the Smell
I make a game of matching smells in the following way:

1. Gather together many small bottles (baby food, prescription).
2. Paint half of the lids red, half blue.
3. Soak cotton balls (two of each) in different flavorings such as vanilla, peppermint, smoke, or lemon. Peanut butter is also good.
4. Put one smell in a red jar and a corresponding smell in a blue jar.

Play by having the child pick one red smell and then find the matching scent in the blue bottles.

Feel and Find
My preschoolers and I play a game we call "feel and find." I have two durable bags, each containing exactly the same things. A child will close his eyes to feel an object. Then his little hand goes into the other bag to find the matching object. Use different textures such as tin foil, cardboard, sandpaper, velvet, and nylon net.

164

Matching Picture Cards

Make matching pictures for mounting on index cards by drawing two objects at the same time, using carbon paper. Make two each of several different things on white paper (apple, flower, star, ship, ball, tree). Glue to cards and play a game with the child by putting three in a row and asking which is different, which are the same. You can also play a "what is missing" game by placing six different cards face up. Remove one at a time, asking him which picture is missing.

Buttons, Buttons

A collection of buttons can be sorted in a variety of ways: according to shape, color, size, or number of holes.

PUPPETS

Finger Puppets
This puppet is simple to make
and easy for small hands to use.
Cut a 4-by-6-inch paper figure
(you and your child can color in
the face and dress) and attach it
to the front of your middle and
index fingers with a rubber
band. The fingers become its
legs. It can run, skip, and dance.

Big Nose
Any kind of face can be drawn
on a small paper bag with small
holes cut out of the front and
two sides. The index finger
pokes through the front hole to
become the puppet's nose, and
thumb and middle fingers
become the arms when poked
through the side holes.

Puppets on a Straw
A puppet can be made by using
a straw with a face from a
magazine picture glued on the
end. A shoebox with a slit in the
bottom is the stage. My children
slip the straw puppet through
the slit and have a puppet show.

166

Use Your Imagination with the Following:

—A small box (from cough drops or candy) can be painted and used as a base for a puppet.

—A small rubber ball can be made into a puppet by digging a hole out of the bottom long enough for index finger.

—A ping-pong ball can become a puppet's head.

—Old gloves make a good base for puppets.

—Figures pasted on a tongue depressor are simple for small hands to manipulate.

—A handkerchief or washcloth can be stuffed and tied with a string.

—Puppets can be made from old socks, apples, or styrofoam.

Second Life for Rubber Toys

Make puppets out of old rubber squeak toys. By cutting around the bottom for hand or fingers to fit in, and adding a bit of ruffled material, you have a cute and familiar puppet.

ART PROJECTS

Good Glue
A good thin white glue for children can be made by combining $\frac{1}{2}$ cup water with $\frac{1}{2}$ cup glue. Save leftover squeeze bottles—one for each child—to be filled with this glue.

Use Wallpaper Paste
I have found wallpaper paste to be most effective for children to use. You can inexpensively mix just what you need or fill and refill squeeze bottles. The new vinyl pastes have an antimildew agent that keeps the paste fresh. It is easily washed out of children's clothes.

Play Dough
Here are three tried and true recipes for play dough:
1. 1 cup baking soda
   $\frac{1}{2}$ cup cornstarch
   $\frac{5}{8}$ cup cold water
2. 1 $\frac{1}{2}$ cups salt
   1 cup cornstarch
   $\frac{1}{2}$ cup water

For either of the above recipes, combine ingredients and cook for about six minutes, until the mixture is about the consistency of mashed potatoes. Spread dough on cookie sheet to cool. Cover and keep moist.
3. 3 cups flour
   1 cup salt
   1 cup water
   1 tablespoon oil

Mix flour and salt. Add water and oil gradually. Knead mixture until it works easily and doesn't stick. Keep refrigerated in plastic bag.

Using the Play Dough
Try some of the following with your child:

—Let children make dough shapes with small cookie cutters.

—Plastic knives and forks are good for cutting and playing with dough.

—Help children make beads of various shapes with holes for stringing. Bake shapes at 200-250 degrees until hard (about two hours) and store for future use.

—Any item hardened in the oven can be painted with poster paints. Apply shellac for a glossy finish. Christmas ornaments are especially nice made from play dough.

—Sometimes before we make the play dough, I let my little ones take the flour sifter, flour, salt, and measuring cups outside to practice sifting and measuring (spread some newspaper down first). When they have had their fill, I put the mixture in a bowl and add the water and oil called for in the recipe.

Homemade Paste
1 ½ cups flour
1 ¼ cups cold water
2 ¾ cups boiling water
1 teaspoon oil of wintergreen
1 teaspoon powdered alum

Stir flour and cold water until smooth. Add boiling water. Cook in double boiler until lumps disappear. Cool. Add remaining ingredients and mix. Store in covered containers.

Flour Paste
1 cup flour
1 teaspoon salt
2 cups water

Stir over medium heat until bubbly and thick. Simmer five minutes. Cool. Refrigerate until used.

Roll-On Paste or Glue
Pry off the ball of a roll-on deodorant. Rinse bottle well. Fill with glue and push ball back in.

Finger Painting

There are not too many things more enjoyable to a young child than to be able to leisurely paint a picture with his hands, swirling and playing in the paint. This type of painting provides a wonderful opportunity for free creative expression. For the finger paints themselves, try adding dry poster paint (commercial) or liquid food coloring to one of the following recipes:

1. For each color, combine $\frac{1}{4}$ cup liquid laundry starch with 2 drops food coloring or 1 teaspoon poster paint.

2. In a 2-quart pan combine $\frac{1}{2}$ cup dry laundry starch and $\frac{1}{2}$ cup cold water. Cook until sticky and hard to stir. Then add, one cup at a time, 4 cups of boiling water. Finally, add 1 teaspoon of glycerine (can be purchased at drugstore). Separate into baby food jars and add 3 drops food coloring or 1 teaspoon dry paint to each jar.

3. Combine $\frac{1}{2}$ cup instant cold water starch, $\frac{1}{2}$ cup soap flakes, and $\frac{5}{8}$ cup (5 ounces) water. Whip this mixture with beaters until it reaches the consistency of whipped potatoes. Add coloring.

Papier-Mache

Make a paste with $3\frac{1}{2}$ cups water, one cup flour, and $1\frac{1}{2}$ tablespoons sugar. Cook over medium heat, stirring constantly, until translucent. Cool. Thin with water if necessary. (Variation: Wallpaper paste, mixed according to package directions, can also be used.) Soak strips of newspaper in paste and crisscross them onto a balloon. Smooth well after each addition. Let dry and paint with poster paints.

Buttermilk Paint

Add color to buttermilk for a nice and new finger-paint consistency.

Finger Painting Paper

The paper for finger painting cannot be very absorbent. White shelf-lining paper is excellent. Preferably the paper should be about 16 x 22 inches. To prepare the paper for the finger paints, draw it quickly through water and place on the table. Add one teaspoon color at a time.

Vinyl Mats

The best idea I have come across in years is to provide a two-foot-square sheet of white oilcloth for each of my children. For finger painting it is terrific because it provides a perfect surface for the paints. When the children are tired the mats are simply rinsed off and stored away until next time.

Other uses for the mats are:
—For rolling out cookies and play dough.
—To cut on.
—To put paper on while painting with water colors.
—Good for most art projects.

Stiff Paint

Whip a mixture of 2 cups soap flakes and ½ cup water together till stiff. Color it or leave it white. Do all sorts of things, such as mash it onto colored paper with fingers, fork, or knife.

Pudding Paint

I have let my children finger paint (with clean hands) with prepared instant pudding. Try it!

Poster Paints

Poster paints are a good medium for children to use. They allow for much creativity. Here are some tips to consider:
—Invest in a few good, wide, 1-inch brushes.
—Give small children a choice of only one or two colors at a time.
—Provide a brush for each color.
—Use large paper (newsprint from a newspaper company is excellent).
—If possible, attach paper to an easel.
—Powder paint in large containers is quite economical. Mix it according to directions and store in baby-food jar.
—A six-cup muffin tin cut in half lengthwise makes two excellent paint holders.
—For extra glossy pictures, mix one tablespoon clear liquid detergent with two tablespoons poster paint.
—A little petroleum jelly around the lip of the paint jar makes it easier to open the next time.

Window Painting

We have a large window in the kitchen. I wet it down first, then give the children each a handful of shaving cream. They make designs or pictures. When they are finished, window cleaner is provided to clean the window.

Bedroom Mural

When my children are at the age when they want to write on the wall, I buy some long butcher paper and tape it all along one wall of their bedroom. They can scribble to their hearts' content, but only on the paper. The older children also enjoy this idea. I let them invite their friends over to help them make murals. These are easily rolled up and stored for keepsakes.

Mat Board

Most art supply and picture framing companies have a box of odd-sized and leftover mat board that is priced inexpensively. I use these pieces for mounting a child's little pictures, for pasting cutouts on, or as backing for a collage.

Buy Good Scissors

After many bad experiences I have learned not to buy cheap scissors for small, inexperienced hands. I spend a little extra and buy a good pair that my child can control. Now he does not get so easily discouraged.

Tie-Dye Designs

Help your child fold a piece of paper towel or napkin over several times. Add liquid color (water colors, poster paints, or food coloring) to the corners. Wait several minutes till napkin absorbs color. Open it up and you have a lovely design.

String Pictures

My children enjoy making string pictures. They dip string in glue and then arrange it on paper to dry into a picture or design.

Cardboard Easel

Three sides of a fairly large box are used. The tops of the upright sides each have two holes. A string is drawn through the corresponding holes on each side and tied. Clothespins or thumbtacks can be used to hold paper in place. Two people can use this easel at once.

Wall Easel

A wall-hung easel can be made by taking a piece of plywood or masonite (about 20 by 26 inches is a good size). Glue a two-inch wooden block onto each bottom corner. Drill a hole in each top corner and hang from wall. The blocks give the easel the desired angle outward from the wall. Glue two clothespins near the top for gripping paper.

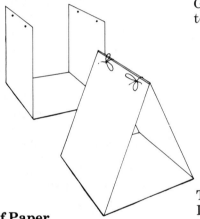

Shelf Paper

White shelf paper hanging on a large paper towel holder low enough for the little ones to reach has become my children's source for art paper. A yardstick for cutting hangs nearby.

Tablecloth to the Rescue

I have an old vinyl tablecloth that the children use when playing with crayons, play dough, paints, or other potentially messy items.

Spaghetti Pictures

Cooked spaghetti can be used to create pictures. Stick it to colored construction paper in different interesting designs. It sticks as it dries.

Eraser Art

Next time your child is drawing with a pencil, show him a new way by having him use the side of the lead to gray in the entire page. Then use the eraser to draw with.

Leaf Rubbings

Leaf rubbings can be made by placing a leaf between two pieces of paper. Crayon rubbed over the top paper allows the shape and veins of the leaf to appear.

Paper by the Mile

My mother goes to a printing shop to get the end paper rolls that are no longer useable for the printer, but still have enough left on them to keep grandchildren in different colored paper for months. Some rolls have been the perfect size to refill empty waxed-paper containers, making it very convenient to tear off the right amount.

Egg Cartons

I save empty egg cartons for my children's art projects. They can be cut to make string mobiles, stacked and painted to make large buildings, or decorated to become treasure boxes for collections of tiny trinkets.

Newsprint

End rolls of newsprint are available at many newspaper companies. On warm days I will roll out wide newsprint across the driveway and let the kids invite friends to help paint or color on it.

IN THE CAR

Name That Tune
My husband will play "Name That Tune" with family members while traveling in the car. He'll whistle a familiar tune. The first to identify it is the winner. The one with the most "wins" is the grand prize winner.

I Spy
"I spy with my little eye" is a popular car game. Someone says, "I spy with my little eye something that begins with 's'." Everyone guesses until the object is named. The winner gets to be the "spy" next.

Travel Kit
I have a travel kit that contains quiet toys and different things to keep the children busy while we are traveling. When we are going to be on the road for several hours I will buy several inexpensive attention getters before we leave, and wrap them as "surprise packages." These may be opened one at a time every 100 miles.

Quiet Cases
Children love suitcases, so I made each of my four children a small case (an old purse will do) filled with special toys. The car was the only place they were allowed to play with it. They were always quiet and seated before I gave it to them, and they usually stayed that way.

Create Riddles

Taking turns making up riddles
is a fun way to help the time
pass while riding in a car. When
you are "it" you get to ask the
question, such as:

1. "What is bright yellow,
tangy, and goes on sandwiches?"
(mustard)

2. "What is brown, sticky,
slips easily through bare toes,
and Mom hates it?" (mud)

3. "I wag my tail and I
rhyme with log: what am I?"
(dog)

Travel Bingo

A favorite game with my family
is travel bingo. The bingo cards
are prepared in advance with
the names of common objects
instead of numbers written in
the squares. (You could also
draw simple pictures for smaller
children.) As the objects are
observed along the way, they are
checked off (or punched). The
first one to fill in a whole line
wins that game.

JUST FOR FUN

Tiny Tot Makeup Bag

I gave my daughter an old purse filled with a comb, mirror, pen and pencil, lip gloss, and wallet. With this and a pair of high heels, she'll play mother for hours.

Clothespins

Clothespins are popular toys in our house. They can be tossed into buckets, or made into dolls or animals by painting faces and clothes on them. Finger exercise is also gained from squeezing the clothespins.

Wallpaper Books

Outdated wallpaper books are available at many paint stores. Kids can paste, cut, and make big scrapbooks or disposable place mats.

Dollhouse

A dollhouse can be made out of an old box. I let my daughter use her imagination to create furniture out of empty spools, match boxes, fabric, foil, lids, buttons, and paper clips. Toothpaste caps make excellent flowerpots. Scissors, glue, and old wallpaper are provided also.

Tea Party

We have a teapot in which I put juice or milk for a juice party. Little dolly sandwiches (any sandwich cut in four pieces) and cookies are given to each guest. These parties are especially enjoyable outside.

Refinished Blackboards

Old, worn-out blackboards no longer need to be thrown away. A spray blackboard finish can be purchased at art supply stores. An inexpensive new blackboard can be created by spraying cardboard or wood with this finish.

Toothbrush

A toothbrush given to a preschooler will clean his teeth as he chews on it.

Shave with Dad

My husband will often put shaving cream on my son so he can look just like Daddy when he shaves. It's easily "shaved off" with a tiny piece of cardboard.

Sticky Fun

Allowing a child to pull apart a large role of masking tape is an inexpensive and "to the rescue" way of keeping him busy when you must have him quiet and still, such as when he is having his picture taken or his hair cut.

Gadgets and Tools

Expensive toys are not always the ones that hold attention and help to teach. My children love a box filled with old nuts and bolts, an old clock without the back (oh! so many screws), an old radio with the back off (minus the cord), and many various old tools.

Nail Board Designs

My child once received an unusual gift of a four-inch square piece of wood with 25 little finished nails hammered in five rows to a height of about half an inch. Included was a package of multicolored rubber bands. The instructions were to create designs by stretching the rubber bands between the nails. He loves it! Yarn of different colors would be fun too.

Outside Fun

An old spray bottle filled with water is used by my three-year-old to water plants, wash wheels on the car, or wash outside walls.

Surprise Bag

I have a babysitter's surprise bag in which I collect all kinds of junk mail, old greeting cards, string, and old clothes. The children love to play with these articles when the babysitter arrives.

Tiny Cookie Cutters

One of my very best purchases has been a box of miniature cookie cutters. The children use them for play dough, and for cutting out cookies. I use them for cutting out little open face sandwiches and finger Jello.

Lock and Key

An inexpensive lock and key will always please a youngster. It's fun and time-consuming as a toy, and a great item to give as a gift.

Cardboard Fun

Because we buy many food items by the case, we usually have several huge boxes. My son appropriates these and uses them for cars, boats, or forts. Often preschoolers are pulled around in the boxes. They love it!

Let's Play Zoo

As a special treat I give my kids a box of animal crackers and let them get out their small blocks or construction paper and scissors. They'll play zoo for hours.

Milk Carton Bowling

Make milk cartons into rectangles by taping the pouring end down with masking tape. Cover, if desired, with paint or colored paper. The cartons are used as bowling pins, and a good-sized rubber ball is rolled to knock them down.

Doctor Kit

Young doctors and nurses love to carry and work with their own old suitcases filled with toy thermometers, raisins for pills, popsicle sticks for tongue depressors, torn sheets for bandages, and sticks for splints. Empty bandage boxes are also used. Dad's discarded white shirts worn backwards make wonderful uniforms.

Water Pail Painting

I give each of my youngsters a pail of water and a large paintbrush and let them paint the sidewalk, bushes, toy cars, tricycles, or outside walls.

Big Pattern Books

My daughter would rather have big pattern books (available at yardage shops) than any paper dolls. She makes her own families and chooses each person's clothes by merely cutting them out. She also has old catalogues from which she can cut out beds, toys, dishes, and everything else she can think of to set up a paper play house.

Miniature Town

A flat box filled with soil can become a miniature town. For example, dirt piled into little hills or roads, moss for grass, a mirror for a pond, and twigs and branches for trees can be used creatively. Let the child use his imagination using such things as little boxes for buildings and toothpicks or matchsticks for fences.

Fun with Junk

Whenever I clean out drawers or cupboards, I save the discards in a box (the things I think the children would enjoy). Sometimes this becomes a "stay-in-bed box" when the children are sick, or sometimes I just let them play with the contents for a few hours or days.

Scoops for Sand

I save all the lids to spray cans so that the children can use them as scoops for the sandbox or wading pool.

Creative Box
I keep a large box filled with a
wide variety of materials for my
children to use. The rule is that
they are free to use whatever
they need from the box for their
projects, providing they return
what they don't use and they
keep the box orderly. They must
clean up after themselves each
time they make something. I
buy many items in quantity at
low prices as they come on sale.
Some items you might want to
include in a box are:
—Waxed paper
—Paper plates
—Lightweight rope
—Paste
—Glue
—Postcards
—Old greeting cards
—Colored construction paper
—Bits of old lace
—String
—Ribbon
—Old stamps or decals
—Wrapping paper
—Crayons
—Finger paints
—Poster paints
—Felt tip pens
—Pencils
—Yarn
—Felt squares
—Scissors
—Recipe cards
—Confetti dots

—Lace doilies
—Paper napkins
—Christmas cards
—Gummed stars
—Tape
—Pipe cleaners
—Lined paper
—Unlined paper
—Aluminum foil
—Toothpicks
—Lightweight cardboard
—Envelopes
—Manila envelopes

Water Play
Many times when I am busy in
the kitchen I will let my little
son stand up to the sink and
play with kitchen utensils in the
water. Funnels, plastic cups,
straws, different-sized
measuring cups, and eggbeaters
are favorites. As his attention
begins to lag I will take the
eggbeater and a little detergent
and whip up lots of soapy suds
for him to play with.

City on the Floor

I used fabric crayons to draw a miniature city on an old sheet. City blocks, lakes, trees, houses, and roads are drawn so that little cars, animals, and people can populate the pretend town.

Driveway Drawing

I allow my children to write with white or colored chalk on the driveway and sidewalks of our house. They know they are responsible for hosing the cement clean when they are through. Sometimes a hopscotch game will go on for two or three days.

"WHAT SHALL WE DO NOW, MOM?"

Here are some answers to the question most frequently asked by children seven to twelve years old.

IDEAS FOR KIDS

Letter Hunt
Go for a walk and don't come back until you have found five things that begin with the letter "L" or any letter you choose.

Buried Treasure
Find something fun around the house (an old toy of yours or a treat) and place it in a box or plastic bag. Then go out to the sandpile and hide it well under the dirt. Invite your younger brothers and sisters to come and dig for it.

Tape Recorder Fun
If Mom says it's okay, play with the tape recorder. Tape a story for a little brother or sister, practice up on your singing voice, or tape songs from the radio.

Parties
With your mother's permission, plan a party. Spend the afternoon making place cards, invitations, and prizes.

Lots of Ways
Find out how many different ways you can draw a tree, a ball, a flower, or a house. Find out how many things you can make from the shape of a circle, a triangle, a square, a diamond, or a rectangle.

Letter Art
Write, in large capitals, each letter of the alphabet. Then turn them into animals, people, or silly objects.

Classy Paper Dolls

Make your own paper dolls out of thin cardboard, white paper, crayons, and glue. Make a beautiful wardrobe for each doll using every style and color you can think of.

Secret Messages

Secret messages can be written with a mixture of $1\frac{1}{2}$ tablespoons of baking soda and $\frac{3}{4}$ cup of warm water. Dip artist's pen into solution and write message. A warm iron over the paper will reveal the secret.

Soap Sculpture

Using a bar of soap and a paring knife, carve yourself a sculpture.

Fetch

Go on a walk and bring back four things that you would like to keep or that you find beautiful.

Pipe Cleaner Menagerie

Using only pipe cleaners, create as many animals as your imagination permits.

Balloon Messages

Write a letter to a friend on the outside of an inflated balloon. Deflate and give it to your friend. Or write a note on a piece of paper, fold it up, and put it inside a balloon. Blow up the balloon and tie it. Your friend will have to pop it to get the message.

Finger Stamps

Using a stamp pad and your fingers, make figures and people from your fingerprints. Caption with comic lines.

Bouncy Ball

Make a bouncing ball by wrapping several rubber bands around a crumpled piece of aluminum foil until it is covered.

Mail

Write letters to friends or send for free booklets.

Wire and Wood
Make a sculpture from fine wire or from small wood scraps or toothpicks and white glue.

Rock House
Some older boys made a rock house by hammering scraps of wood together in the shape of a house. They spent hours gluing rocks on it and shellacking over it for a nice shine.

Double Image
Fasten two different-colored felt tip pens together with a rubber band or string. One must be pushed down in order to be longer than the other. Make double-image lettering or art projects.

Magic
Get a book on magic from the library and learn some tricks, perhaps two or three at which you can become expert.

Play Telephones
Old tried-and-true standbys are often fun. For example, make play telephones from two paper cups connected by a long string. The string should be about 25 to 40 feet long so that it can stretch from one room to another. If children have trouble hearing each other at first, check to make sure the string is pulled tightly.

Yarn Game
Take turns holding a three-foot piece of yarn high and letting it float to the floor. Each child has thirty seconds to decide what the shape looks like.

Soldering
Learn how to use and what you can do with a soldering iron.

"What Shall We Do Now?" "I Don't Know."

When you and your friend can't decide what to do next you might do what my oldest daughter and her best friend always did. Each would take a sheet of paper and make a list of every possible thing they could think of to do. Then they would take turns eliminating the possibilities one by one, and they would do whatever was left last on the list.

New Twist on Old Game

Find a game you've played often and sit down and invent a new way to play it.

Gift Stationery

From plain white paper and various materials such as small feathers, bits of lace, string, sequins, and colored ink pens, create your own personalized stationery. Use it for your own letter writing or make a gift for a friend.

Make a Mobile

Use your imagination and make a mobile out of anything you can think of. Fishing line or transparent sewing thread are both good to use. Consider such items as driftwood, aluminum foil, pieces of lightweight wood cut into various shapes and painted, waxed paper shapes with crayons pressed between, or colored construction paper cut into snowflakes.

Greeting Cards

From the materials used in the gift stationery plus old wrapping paper and colored construction paper, make a box of handmade greeting cards. Make all kinds: Birthday, Congratulations, Get Well, I Love You, and Christmas.

Juggle

Get three oranges, tennis balls, rubber balls, or similar objects and try your hand at juggling.

Simple Games
Don't forget simple games, like marbles, Scrabble, pick-up-sticks, dominoes, tiddly winks, Bingo, jacks, or Chinese checkers.

Charades
Learn to play charades. Your friends will really love to play. It's fun anywhere and anytime.

Water Balloons
Nothing is more fun than an all-out water balloon fight on a hot summer day.

Rainbow
Count how many colors there are in the garden.

Hopscotch
Draw a hopscotch game on the driveway with chalk.

Place Cards
Make place mats or place cards for tonight's dinner.

Poor Folks' Frisbee
Make your own Frisbee by cutting a wedge out of a round piece of cardboard.

Ice Sculpture
During the summer, have Mom freeze a block of ice in a milk carton for you and a friend. Make ice sculptures with a pick and hammer. Or make your sculpture from styrofoam.

Clouds
How many faces and shapes can you find in the clouds?

Nutty Cups
Decorate little paper cups for nut cups either as an after-dinner treat or as a party favor. Lots of fun for a family home evening treat.

More Books
Go to the library and check out an interesting book.

Make Puzzles

Make puzzles for yourself or for smaller children by gluing magazine pictures to thin cardboard and cutting them into interesting shapes.

Mural

Tape a long strip of butcher paper or newsprint along a wall. Invite some friends over and make a wall mural.

Fabric Painting

Paint a picture on paper with fabric crayons. These are made by Crayola and are available at toy and fabric stores. Choose any light-colored fabric (unbleached muslin is good) and transfer the picture permanently to the fabric using the instructions on the crayons.

Summer Sledding

How about flattening a big sturdy cardboard box and making sleds for grassy hill sliding?

Kitchen Creations

Have your mother set out small amounts of various baking ingredients, including flour, soda, baking powder, butter, eggs, salt, and sugar. You and a friend or brother or sister combine the ingredients without a recipe into something wonderful. This is a good way to learn what the different ingredients are for and also to learn the necessity of following directions.

Clay Contest

Make salt clay and have a contest with a friend to see who can make the most things in twenty minutes.

Used Books

Go with Mom to a garage sale, junk store, or used book store and get some inexpensive treasures of books. Children's books written at the turn of the century are excellent because they stress high values and morals.

Spray Gun Cowboys
Use spray bottles for a lively backyard game of Cowboys and Indians.

Some Quick Ideas
—Have a pogo-stick jumping contest.
—Make paper airplanes and have a flying contest.
—Ask Mom to help you create a makeup kit for experimenting.
—Put together a jigsaw puzzle.
—Have a bubble-gum blowing contest.
—Wash the family car.
—Play musical chairs with the neighborhood kids.
—Paint with small brushes and water colors.
—Make something with wood, hammer, and nails.
—Go fly a kite. Make one first.

Dishcloth Needlework
Use a mesh dishcloth, twine, and a tapestry needle and try some needlework.

Parachutes
Punch holes in each corner of a small square cut from an old sheet. Tie cords of the same length to each. Gather the ends of all four cords to attach to a fishing weight. Toss the parachute and watch it open and float slowly down.

Plastic Lid Fun
Use old plastic lids—the bigger the better. Make pictures on them. Use them as Frisbees. Have a race rolling them.

Sleep Outdoors
Set up a tent (either a real one or one made from old sheets) in the backyard. Invite a friend over to sleep outdoors.

PLANT SOMETHING AND WATCH IT GROW

Sweet Potato
Choose a sweet potato with lots of eyes. Place it uncut in a large vase or jar. Toothpicks will hold it so that only the bottom of the potato touches the water. Put it in a place where there is lots of sun. Soon you will see sprouts and then leaves. Sometimes this may take six to eight weeks, but eventually you will have a very lovely plant that can continue to be grown in water or potted in soil.

Grass Seed
Sprinkle seed on a damp sponge. Keep the sponge nice and damp for a few days and see what happens.

Vegetables
You can grow a small box of lettuce on a sunny windowsill. It starts very quickly and is fun to watch. Also, try a container of radishes. They take only three weeks from seed to harvest.

Celery
Put the inside part of a celery bunch (the heart and some leaves) in a glass filled with water.

Lentils
Place lentils in a shallow dish of sand or soil, and in just a few days they will sprout into lovely greens that will last for several weeks.

Lima Beans

Soak beans overnight in water.
Plant in soil in a paper cup.
Another interesting way to
watch beans grow is to place one
between a damp paper towel
inside a glass jar. As it sprouts
you can watch the roots form.

Pineapple Top

Cut the top off a ripe pineapple.
Pull the bottom leaves out and
allow the top to dry for a day.
Then place it in a shallow bowl
of pebbles or sandy soil. Be
patient, and eventually new
growth will appear on the top.

Carrot

Remove leaves from the top of
the carrot and cut it one-half
inch from the top. Then put it in
a shallow dish of sand. Keep the
sand damp and put it in strong
sunlight. It will produce pretty,
green, fernlike foliage.

Windowsill Flowers

Choose a flower that doesn't
grow too tall and yet is fast
growing. Marigolds and alyssum
are two favorites. They will both
bloom beautifully on a sunny
windowsill. Plant in a good
packaged potting soil.

Coleus

This is a beautiful houseplant
that has red and green leaves. It
is easy to grow from seed. Buy a
package of seed and plant in a
good potting soil. Place in a
sunny window. (The sunnier the
window, the brighter the colors
in the leaves will be.)

Lemons, Oranges, Grapefruit

Citrus seeds are easy to grow.
Pick out some of the largest
seeds and plant them several to
a pot. After you know they have
sprouted and are coming up,
allow only one plant to a pot.
These plants won't have fruit on
them, but they all have very
pretty, shiny leaves and make
attractive plants.

Grapevine
Did you know that you can
plant the seeds from a little
grape and they will grow into a
plant that can be trained to
grow along a window or on a
trellis? Plant two or three seeds
in a small pot. Keep damp in a
sunny place till they are growing
well.

BE CURIOUS—FIND OUT:

How to Make Rain
Allow steam from a kettle to
condense inside a glass held
over the spout.

How a Plant Drinks Water
Pick a light-colored flower (a
white carnation is very good)
and place it in a glass of colored
water (use food coloring). What
happened? You might also try
cutting the top off a carrot and
placing it in colored water. Try
putting a stalk of celery in a
different color and then cutting
open the carrot and celery stalk
the next day. What happened?

If Air Is a "Thing"
Stuff a handkerchief into the
bottom of a glass. Plunge the
glass upside down in water. The
handkerchief will remain dry
because of the layer of air
between it and the water.

How a Compass Works
Rub a needle on a magnet. Then
put a little oil on the needle and
float it in water. The needle
should point north.

SHARE YOUR SUCCESSES

Dear reader:

This project has been exciting and most rewarding for us. We know that there still exists among you an untapped reservoir of strength, experience, and knowledge. As you read through this book, new ideas and your own successes will undoubtedly come to mind. It is our hope that as they do, you will share them with us, that this may be an ongoing resource, filling a need in the lives of mothers everywhere. Send your ideas to:

The Family Idea Book
Editorial Department
Deseret Book Company
P.O. Box 30178
Salt Lake City, UT 84130

INDEX